GOD'S HAND
in the
HIMALAYAS

AND OTHER SHORT STORIES

GARY SHEPHERD

D0104573

Wycliffe

AUSTRALIA

GOD'S HAND IN THE HIMALAYAS

ISBN: **978-0-9871972-0-7**

Unless otherwise indicated, Bible quotations are taken from The New International version of the Bible, copyright 1973, 1978 by New York International Bible Society, and The Holy Bible, New King James version copyright 1982, 1994 by Thomas Nelson, Inc.

Book Cover

Design by:

Michael and Sarah Shepherd

The top picture is of Baju, Michael and Adina's village grandfather. A Magar lady has brought her sick baby to him for healing.

To my knowledge, in the early 1970s Baju was the only indigenous believer living in that part of the Kali Gandaki River basin. At that time, the nearest church consisted of a handful of beleaguered Christians clustered around the Tansen Mission Hospital. This town is situated on the crest of the Mahabharat Range, a 24-hour trek west of Arakhala.

Despite continued harassment and persecution by government officials and religious leaders of the day, Baju refused to be intimidated. Like an old prophet of ancient times, he stood solid as a rock, faithfully proclaiming the Word of God. In Jesus' name he would freely pray for all who came to him whether in private or in public.

The bottom picture is a view from Arakhala Village. Michael and Adina's mother, Barbara, is seen looking northward across the fog-filled valleys towards the panorama of the mighty Himalayas.

Barbara Joan Shepherd
(November 5, 1942 - December 3, 1991)

DEDICATED

⌘

To the memory of

Barbara Joan Shepherd
a devoted follower of Jesus Christ

My first wife, Barbara, committed her life to Jesus at a young age. In her teenage years she felt God leading her to a lifetime of missionary service. She graduated at the top of her class from Simpson Bible College and San Diego State University. She was an accomplished musician who set aside a career in music to live a life of hardship and simplicity in a remote corner of the world. Above all, she had a servant heart. She was a devoted wife and mother. Without her help the Magar New Testament would not have happened.

For many, many years Barbara expended a large amount of time and energy to care for the sick and needy who came to our door. She readily prayed for those who were suffering and in need. Not unusually she would be called to a villager's home to treat someone in critical condition. Her welcoming smile, and her love and compassion for the Magar people was deeply appreciated. As a result, when the Magars built a road into their area after her death, it was named, "Barbara Road," in honor of her.

PREFACE

To maintain the privacy of certain individuals, the names of some people and places have been changed.

I am grateful to Peter Schmideche, Alice Brown, Jenny Evans, and Marilyn Ford for offering their valuable suggestions as well as to Dayle Fergusson and Margy Mitton for editing the final manuscript.

We are indebted to Harrold Andresen for writing chapter 19, regarding the circumstances of Barbara's funeral.

Above all, I am most thankful for my wife, Kerry, who has been so patient with me through the years. She has always encouraged me and has endured wonderfully through the long preparation of this manuscript. She listened and read through my stories a number of times, offering many good ideas to more accurately portray the contents.

I was able to refer back to letters I had written at the time when many of these stories occurred. Apologies are offered where lapse of memory on my part may be responsible for any misrepresentation of fact. My sincere thanks are offered to the Magar people for sharing their lives with me and my family.

CONTENTS
❧❦

ix

An Illiterate Old Magar Lady

Two Stories from the 1980s

My Time of Great Loss (1991-1992)

New Beginnings with that Nurse (1992-2003)

Peatam – Baju's Disciple (1995-2003)

More of God's Astonishing Power

INTRODUCTION

❧

God's Hand in the Himalayas is the second book in a series of true stories which began with *Angel Tracks in the Himalayas*. These stand-alone short stories were originally written for my grandchildren at the request of my daughter, Adina. For many of these stories, I was able to refer back to letters that I had written at the time.

If you have read *Angel Tracks*, you will have met Baju, my faithful friend and language helper who became the most outstanding Christian I have known. In this book you will also meet Peatam, one of my son Michael's childhood friends. He was with Baju when he passed away in 1996. Just like Elisha received Elijah's anointing, Peatam seems to have received Baju's powerful anointing.

I grew up on Whidbey Island in Washington State, not far from the Canadian border. We lived in the small rural town of Oak Harbor where my father was a businessman and my mother a school teacher. My life revolved around sports and outdoor activities, particularly hunting and fishing. For many years the Boy Scouts, in which I earned the Eagle Scout award, formed an important part of my life. In 1963, I graduated from the University of Washington with a degree in business and joined the U.S. Navy as an officer through the ROTC program. There on my ship I began to read the Bible for the first time. After sixteen months of searching, I was led to devote my life to Jesus and to follow His ways for the rest of my life.

My first wife, Barbara, grew up in La Mesa, a suburb of San Diego, California. She graduated at the top of her class from San Diego State University with a degree in education. She was a first grade school teacher who also excelled in music. She participated wholeheartedly in our adventures in Nepal until her tragic death in 1991.

Our daughter, Adina, was born in Nepal in 1971. She and her brother, Michael, who was born in 1973, grew up among the Magars, a people of oriental origins. Both of them became native speakers of the Magar and Nepali languages. Adina is now a pastor's wife living in Abilene, Texas. Among many things, she is involved in grief counseling. Michael is a senior engineer for Dell, Inc. His responsibilities include a focus on memory chip development. He lives with his family in Leander, Texas.

My wife, Kerry, is from Melbourne, Australia. I first met her in Kathmandu, Nepal after Barbara's death. She had been working for a number of years as a missionary nurse in various parts of the country. You will meet her in Chapter 24.

Nepal is a narrow, mountainous country stretching out for 660 miles along the Himalayas. It is sandwiched between India on the south and the Tibetan Plateau on the north. An ancient people called Magars live in the rugged mountains between the mighty Himalayas and the Indian plains. Some tribes have oral histories which tell of their wanderings and settlement in Nepal. The Magars, however, have been in Nepal for so long that I was unable to find anyone who could relate such stories. This leads me to believe that they were among the original settlers of the land.

Our friends, and particularly our children's friends, were frequently dying from one disease or another. We could and did help the villagers to overcome that. Often, if not annually, there was a severe food shortage, and sometimes outright famine. We could and did help them to significantly produce more food. But the great spiritual oppression they lived under was another thing.

For nearly two hundred years, the British Empire has recruited soldiers from the mountains of Nepal. Their experience revealed that the finest came from four tribes: the Magar, Gurung, Rai and Limbu. These men were the strongest of the strong, the most faithful of the faithful, and the bravest of the brave. Consequently, it seemed to be a contradiction that back in their own villages some of these brave men would be so fearful of the dark spirit forces. In fact, the Magars lived in great spiritual bondage which affected all areas of their lives.

If their crushing spiritual oppression was broken, they might be open to changing the ways that resulted in such poverty and poor health. Our method of teaching was to model with our lives rather than with words. If someone asked us why, unlike themselves, we did not expend huge amounts of money constantly sacrificing to the spirits, then we would explain. But rather than establishing mere religious doctrine, we wanted them to discover for themselves a friendship with Jesus. Therefore, one of our goals was to translate the New Testament into the Magar language. Then, they themselves could make up their own minds regarding what Jesus taught, and they would be free to apply it in ways that best fit their culture.

For forty-two years, my family and I have been involved with the wonderful Magar people. Our family feels truly fortunate to have lived side by side with some amazing people. Though appearing to be nothing more than backward peasants, some of them are real heroes.

May those who read these stories be encouraged to trust in God's power, and His kindness and unfailing love to those who commit themselves to following Him. They are offered here as an encouragement for Christians who want to apply the teachings of Jesus to their present life situations.

—Stories of God's Power—

CHAPTER 1

GOD'S HAND — LEOPARD ATTACK

స్త్రీ

O my Strength, I watch for You…
O my Strength, I sing praise to You…
Psalm 59:9, 17

Tuesday, May 15, 2003

A bandoned by his village friends, the skinny little weakling didn't stand a chance. The enraged leopard on his back could easily kill a full-grown bull.

Down the mountain and across the stream from Arakhala Village is a steep ridge upon which the village of Danthok lies. Gyan had been the only believer down there but when Gyan's parents, as well as his nephew, became followers of Jesus, it was finally too much.

Some three years earlier the village leaders had decided to put an end to it all. They ordered Gyan and his nephew to sign a paper. It required them to relinquish their allegiance to Jesus Christ and return to their former

3

practice of ancestor and idol worship. When they refused to recant, the villagers beat them and ran them out of the village. Their home, fields, and livelihood were abandoned. They lost nearly everything.

Perched on that same ridge, hardly fifteen minutes walk away, is the little village of Pipalchap. There, from a destitute family lives a seventeen-year-old young man called Looka Bahadur. He is so undersized that people gave him the nickname *Kencya*, meaning the puny or scrawny one.

To add to his pitiful existence, Scrawny contracted a severe case of osteomyelitis, an infection of the bone which ate away half of the shinbone on his right leg. For the past three years, Gyan had been bringing Scrawny into Pokhara and even taking him to Kathmandu for multiple operations and continued treatment. For months at a time, at no small cost to himself, Gyan had cared for him. Subsequently, Scrawny's leg and his life were saved… but just barely.

Not long ago, Scrawny returned to his home a believer... the only one on that friendless ridge since Gyan and his family had been expelled. Like most of those who have followed this course, Scrawny has been under constant pressure to abandon the teachings of Jesus. The small group of believers in the area, however, has been encouraging Scrawny to hang on. They know that if one person can persevere for just a few years in a village, others will eventually find the courage to join him on the Way.

Last Thursday, however, a tragedy was in the making. In the dark of night, a seven-foot leopard crept silently into Pipalchap and stole a pig. Pigs squeal dreadfully when a leopard is carrying them off, so everyone in the village knew exactly what was happening. Early Friday morning all the men were called out to track it down. Some thirty men, carrying sixteen old muzzle-loaders along with two hunting dogs, gathered together. The dogs, wearing tinkling bells around their necks, immediately picked up the scent.

Not far from the village they came upon the leopard. Some of the men shot at it, and I was told that they missed with their primitive weapons. If unhurt, a leopard tries his utmost to escape. Once wounded, however, he sets his heart on revenge. Evidently, this one seemed to have been slightly injured.

The men tracked the killer to the trunk of a huge, hollow tree that had fallen beside a ravine. The hunters surrounded the tree and three of them—including Scrawny—went to see if he was still there. Scrawny, without so much as a stick in his hand, was the last to have a look. The cavity went quite deep into the tree trunk and peering intently into the darkness, Scrawny could just barely make out the big cat.

Suddenly there was a terrifying roar. The man standing beside Scrawny leaped over Scrawny's bent-over body and ran. Jerking his head out of that black hole, Scrawny spun around to dash away. But in a single bound, the leopard caught hold of the tops of Scrawny's shoulders and drove him into the ground.

I once read a book featuring multiple photographs of a leopard battling a fully-mature water buffalo. The massive bull tried every trick to throw the leopard off, including rolling in the stream, but the powerful cat quickly wore him down. He effortlessly avoided the long horns and with seemingly little exertion soon killed the huge buffalo.

Hunters tracking a leopard

Every time I have been called out to hunt leopards with the villagers, the leader of the hunt has always given us strict instructions before we started. Of paramount importance was this mandate: if one of us were attacked, everyone else should rush to his aid. He absolutely forbade us to shoot, for as likely as not, our companion would be hit. The leopard might tear and bite us all, but together with our sickle-knives and sticks we were to drive the leopard away and save our friend's life.

Poor Scrawny was not so fortunate. In his village, the hunters received no such instructions. The leopard standing on his back grasped his head in its jaws. Three times, Scrawny heard the sound of those long fangs grating against his skull. The furious 120 pound beast stood on a helpless 80 pound boy.

A leopard lives by killing. He is a clever and efficient killing machine, renowned for his strength and skill. So one might have expected this powerful animal to seize Scrawny by the back of his skinny little neck and crunch his vertebrae into pieces, killing him instantly. But it didn't... or couldn't.

Instead of piercing or crushing Scrawny's skull, those fangs slipped across the top of his head, ripping back a hand-sized flap of scalp. And just above his neck, a lower fang tore away another three-inch long triangle.

But what about the thirty village men? Not one attacked the leopard. They all stood at a distance screaming at it. One man came close, but he only waved his hand at the animal.

When all had abandoned him, nevertheless, there was One who had not. Face down on the side of that ravine with a raging leopard on his back, Scrawny found himself suddenly infused with a mighty strength. Convulsing, or bucking like a horse, he threw the leopard into the ravine.

In doing so, Scrawny flipped over and ended lying face up on the slope. In a single bound, the cat was upon him again. Claws tore at his face and great fangs reached in to seize his throat. However, before those long teeth plunged into his neck, Scrawny realized his hands were on the animal's chest. Though helpless and alone, yet again, a great power surged through his puny frame. With a tremendous thrust he catapulted the killer back into the ravine!

That was enough for the leopard. He quickly scurried back into the hollow tree from whence the hunters of Pipalchap soon dispatched him. Scrawny found medical help nearby, and when he was able to walk a couple of days later, he came to Pokhara for further treatment.

As Kerry cleaned his wounds at our house, I questioned him about the incident. My mind couldn't help comparing him to Arnold Schwarzenegger in *The Terminator*, or to the heroes in *Raiders of the Lost Ark* and *Star Wars*... all products of computer graphics, trick photography and fake illusions.

In stark contrast, here was one who had only recently "leaned his heart" upon Jesus. His leg still oozed pus, and fresh claw marks scarred his face. One claw had ripped from the corner of his eye across the bridge of his nose, but providentially had missed his eyeball. Forty-five sutures on his head closed up the long gashes in his scalp. Here, we were privileged to see, was the real deal. God's *strength made perfect in weakness* (2 Corinthians 12:9). It was probably not unlike what the shepherd boy, young King David, experienced when he seized the lion and the bear and killed them (1 Samuel 17:34-37).

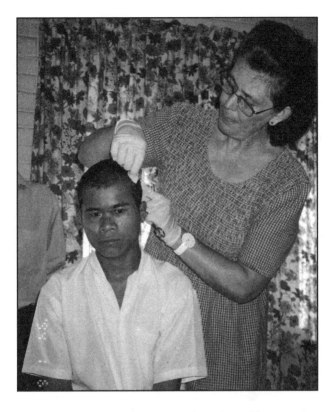

Kerry removing the 45 stitches

This story, however, didn't occur two or three thousand years ago. It was an event that had happened that very week. It was one that was patently verifiable by thirty eyewitnesses. It was an example and testimony of God's loving care and mighty hand in the Himalayas.

I love you, O LORD, my strength…
He rescued me from my powerful enemy.
Psalm 18:1, 17

—Postscript—

Scrawny continued faithfully as the only believer in his village. In the summer of 2006, he and two other believers from another village delivered a twenty-year-old girl from two years of horrifying demonic bondage. Subsequently, she attended the YWAM Discipleship Training course and returned home at Christmas with a story to tell. Her father was the headman of Pipalchap and the chief leader of the surrounding villages. In March 2007, he boldly asked to be publicly baptized. Including her mother, there are now four believers in Pipalchap Village.

To the faithful you show yourself faithful.
Psalm 18:25

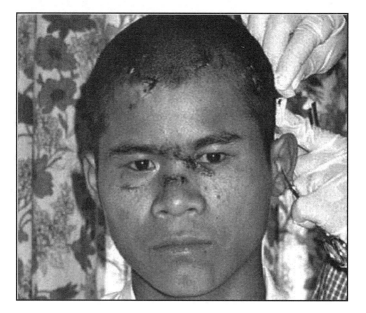

CHAPTER 2

SNAKEBITE

☙❧

I have given you authority to trample on
snakes and scorpions,
and to overcome all the power of the enemy;
nothing will harm you.
Luke 10:19

The snake blended in perfectly with its surroundings and Prem did not see it. Now it was too late. The deadly viper had sunk its fangs deep into his bare foot!

Swiftly, the powerful poison began its lethal work, and within seconds Prem's body was reeling from the violent assault. Almost immediately his lymph glands were overwhelmed as they feebly attempted to deal with this attack on his life. With every beat of his heart Prem felt a surge of increasing pain in his groin and under his arms.

King cobras, kraits, and a number of other poisonous snakes are indigenous to the mountains and valleys of the Magar homeland. Those who are bitten suffer terribly, and have faint hope for a happy ending. The most common snakebite is from the smallish green viper. Its venom regularly kills children and smaller women. The larger and healthier people may survive, but often they are left with a paralyzed limb.

That morning, Prem had taken his small herd of cows down into the deep ravines to graze near the stream. How was he going to make it back up to his little grass hut? How could he manage to climb that steep mountain now? Except for his cows, Prem was all alone. Furthermore, that very morning his wife, Darima, had gone off to visit her relatives, leaving him to look after everything. Even if somehow he did make it home, who would—or who could—help him then?

It had only been a few years since Prem had first "leaned his heart" upon Jesus, and he had paid an exceptionally heavy price for that decision. The beatings and persecution, however, had built a strong foundation of faith in God and His Word. Somewhere in that Book were those words about the followers of Jesus who overcame the venom of a viper (Acts 28:3-6). Today, he would find out whether his considerable investment, through suffering, had earned him that dividend as well.

Snakes are regarded as gods by the Hindus and are rarely killed. But the snake which bit Prem, had picked the wrong person. It died right then and there when Prem pummeled it with his staff. Sitting down next to the dead snake, he placed his hands on his foot. He had prayed for others… often with marvelous results. Even so, usually there was Darima or others who joined with him to pray for the person in need. Now he was alone, and he had never prayed for a snakebite victim.

Today, it would be him and God. He was very alone in that forest. Entirely alone. What was God's plan? What would his Heavenly Father do?

Prem put his hand over the fang marks and began to pray. Immediately, he felt the effect. The spreading pain began to slowly, yet steadily be reversed… almost as if it were being sucked or siphoned right out of the puncture holes. Before long, the pain had completely subsided. When Prem returned home that afternoon, his neighbors wouldn't believe that he had been bitten. That is, until they saw the two puncture wounds in his foot. Other than that, he was none the worse.

This experience, Darima told me, was the beginning of their acquisition of "snakebite medicine." Prem and Darima's gift of healing prayer was already widely known. Now this news of his dealing with the snake also spread to surrounding villages.

One summer day, Prem was resting in his hut because the soles of his feet had deteriorated badly. He had been working far too long in the thick mud of their rice fields and his feet had become so severely split and cracked that he was scarcely able to stand up for the pain.

At this most unpropitious time, someone arrived from a village a few hours walk away. His son had been bitten by a snake and he had come to ask Prem to go and pray. Prem declined, of course, noting the horrible condition of his feet. They were far too painful to walk on. Darima, however, wouldn't let him off that easily. "Can't" was not a word that she associated with following Jesus. In no uncertain terms, she told Prem to get up and go pray. "God will take care of the pain and give you whatever strength you need to get there," she insisted.

Darima had probably calculated that since God was going to take care of the deadly snake venom in someone's leg, it would be no imposition for Him to look after her husband's two cracked feet as well. Prem did make it across the mountains and did pray for the snakebite victim. And indeed, even though the poison had already done considerable damage, the young man recovered rapidly and was even able to go work in his fields the next day.

Then there was another man who lived in Nagar Danda, a village not so far away. One day he came to visit his relatives who lived next door to Prem and Darima. That very night, this fellow stepped on a snake which was lying right outside the door.

He was in a dreadful predicament. The pain in his body was ever increasing and he had no help. There was nowhere to turn. The nearest medical facility was across the mountains, a full day's travel away. It was pitch dark and no one was going to carry him over those dangerous trails until morning light. In addition, there was no shaman in Chainpur Village who might call upon his familiar spirits for help. Fortunately for him, however, his relative took him to the harassed and harried Christians. There, Prem and Darima's God took care of the venom… at no cost.

—Postscript—

One day, Darima's granddaughter was working in the rice fields with some other girls when one of her companions was bitten. Remembering what her grandparents had done, she prayed and the girl was healed on the spot.

The healing process for snakebite, I was told, seemed to happen pretty much the same in every case. After prayer, the pain would begin to decline in that part of the body that was farthest from the bite. It seemed as if the poison was being drained out towards the place of the bite. In the following years, all those bitten by snakes and who came to Prem and Darima returned home healed. Those who went to the shamans or the medical facilities often did not survive.

Darima and her husband have faithfully endured all manner of persecution over the years. In retrospect, Darima once told me, these trials were just times that God was "pulling the weeds" out of their lives. The result of getting rid of the "weeds" was that one day, God gave them snakebite medicine.

And these signs will accompany those who believe…
when they drink deadly poison,
it will not hurt them at all;
they will place their hand on sick people,
and they will get well.
Mark 16:17-18

CHAPTER 3

TOO-MEE-YANG

ॐ‍ॐ

Freely you have received, freely give.
Matthew 10:8

The young shaman watched intently as the blood poured out of me. Greatly alarmed, he wondered how I would survive. He himself would surely die, he declared, if he were to lose that much blood!

The shaman had done all that he could to save his little daughter, but her health had continued to slowly deteriorate. At five years of age, she weighed only eighteen pounds and quite literally was nothing but skin and bones. Now as a last resort to save her life, Ross had brought Bhabikan the shaman and Too-mee-yang his daughter to Shanta Bhawan Hospital in Kathmandu.

The doctor at the mission hospital discovered that she was suffering from several parasites. By far the most insidious was Leishmaniasis, also known as Kala-Azar or Black Fever. For untreated cases of Leishmaniasis, the fatality rate is ninety percent.

The child had become so anemic and desperately weak that Dr. Nitschke was doubtful that she would live long enough for the slow-acting medicine to make any difference. Then an idea came to her. If Too-mee-yang could somehow get a blood transfusion, the little girl just might survive long enough for the medicine to make a difference.

For the past two years our New Zealand friends, Ross and Kathleen Caughley, had been working with the Chepang people. They were an extremely poor tribe that depended heavily on hunting and gathering for survival. Their villages were located in a mountainous region adjacent to that of the Magars. In his search for someone to teach him this strange new language, Ross discovered that Bhabikan was better than anyone else in the village.

As it so happened, Barbara and I were in Kathmandu when Ross and Bhabikan arrived on May 27, 1971. For some reason we weren't going back out to the village for a little while. Ross and I had a blood type that was a match for Too-mee-yang and that is why we were now giving blood. I, a complete stranger, someone from the other side of the world, was offering my blood in a final attempt to preserve the life of this little waif. It was something that her father would never do... for he was absolutely certain it would cost him his own life.

Kathleen, with their two little boys, had been left behind in their remote village, and Ross had to get back to them as soon as he could. So Barbara and I readily agreed to look after Bhabikan. He slept on the floor of his daughter's hospital room and every day I took Barbara up there on the back of our little 90 cc Honda motorcycle. When Too-mee-yang turned the corner and her stomach could manage it, we began bringing boiled eggs and oranges to supplement her diet.

Bhabikan and Too-mee-yang in the hospital

After two or three weeks, Too-mee-yang was released from the hospital and she and her father stayed at our house while travel arrangements were made to send them back. This was our opportunity to be an example of Christ's love. Ross and Kathleen were making all the difficult sacrifices to help the Chepang people, and we felt it a privilege to make this small investment in their efforts.

—Postscript—

While Bhabikan was staying with us, I learned about the terrible fears that shamans often live with. The Chepang shamans fight with one another for territorial control almost continuously. Night after night he had to take out his drum and call up his spirits to do battle. Without their active protection, the spirits of the other shamans would kill him. It was an exhausting life and sometimes they would fight the whole night through.

The following year, Bhabikan became the first person in the Chepang tribe to follow Jesus. Too-mee-yang recovered fully, grew up, and married. At the age of forty she passed away from a liver disease, perhaps related to her original illness. She left behind a legacy of six children raised in a family filled with the love of Jesus and free from the fear of witches or demonic spirits.

Let us not become weary in doing good,
for at the proper time we will reap a harvest
if we do not give up.
Galatians 6:9

CHAPTER 4

THE PUNJABI

*You prepare a table for me in the presence
of my enemies.*
Psalm 23:5

"**I**f your God is so great, let Him feed you!" the
jailers taunted.

Kept in a lonely cell like animals in a pen, the young
shaman and his three friends suffered quietly for eight
long days. School teachers in their village had reported
these new Christians to the authorities. "Never turn them
loose!" they demanded when the police had come to seize
them.

Yes, they were truly guilty. Bhabikan and his friends
had no excuses, no extenuating circumstances whatsoever. They had stopped giving the required blood
sacrifices to their idols and ancestral spirits, and they had
asked Jesus to come into their hearts to guide their lives.

Now there was no one to call upon and no other help
than the name of Jesus. That Name, however, was an
anathema to the police and the prisoners were strictly

forbidden the comfort of praying with one another. That Name epitomized a foreign god... the white people's religion!

As for food, he couldn't claim they weren't fed, Bhabikan told me. However, the few times they were given rice, it was the black scrapings from the bottom of the pot, or else it was old and sour... inedible. Strangely, however, their skinny frames didn't feel the lack of food. Indeed, they all felt as if God had invisibly fed them, he said.

Then on the eighth day, God sent them a cellmate... a truck driver. This unfortunate fellow was a Sikh who had been involved in a traffic accident and someone had been killed. Tragedies like these were always a great opportunity for the police. They would prosper nicely before the driver would get his freedom.

The homeland of the Sikhs is in the Punjab region of India, and consequently, the Chepang people just call them Punjabis. In those times, there were not many heavy vehicles in Nepal and it was the Sikhs, complete with turbans and full beards, who drove the buses and trucks. They moved people and goods across Nepal's few mountain roads, and their service was crucial to the nation's economy. By Nepal village standards, these drivers were very well paid and considered rich.

In appearance, the contrast couldn't have been greater. God has endowed most of the Sikh men with large, heavily-built physiques, and they are widely known as brave and fearless warriors. The Chepangs on the other hand, are an oppressed and timid people. They are poorer and smaller in frame than any other people I know in Nepal. Furthermore, they are of oriental ancestry and the men have very little facial hair. So it must have made an interesting sight: this thickly-bearded, muscular Punjabi could easily have been more than twice the size of the largest of these skinny new believers.

When the Punjabi driver was hungry, he would write a note and instruct a boy to bring him a meal from a nearby eatery. I suppose that this driver was so focused on solving his own crisis that he didn't pay any attention to the gaunt little fellows suffering along in silence. On the third day, however, just as he started to dig into his meal, he noticed his cellmates just sitting there.

"What are you eating?" he inquired.

"Nothing. We have no money," they replied.

Immediately he wrote another note and ordered four more plates of food. Then he asked what they had done and why they were there. He learned that they had been beaten, stripped of their meager clothing, and thrown in jail on account of that Name.

It seems that he was a religious man, for he purchased four new shirts and four pairs of half-length pants for the young men. Furthermore, this mockery of justice outraged the Punjabi and at every opportunity he began to berate the police. "I am here accused of a crime, but these men are here on account of their religion!" he would assert.

This man would have been superior to those policemen in wealth, as well as in physical size. No doubt they had hoped to milk him for all they could over the accident. If he got too upset, the bribe money they would share at his release might substantially dry up. In any case, Punjabi men are intimidating just to look at and no one wanted to get on their wrong side. That could get you seriously hurt!

Whatever their reasoning, the Punjabi fed Bhabikan and his friends three more times before the police capitulated to his demand for justice. When the Chepangs were released, not only did they get their old clothes back, but the few rupees that had been taken away from them were also returned. That was enough money for the bus fare to get them back home.

—Postscript—

Bhabikan received a broken rib as a result of those beatings by the police. Over the years, he was arrested and jailed a total of nine times for his faith. These occasions always included a beating as well. Though the Chepangs are especially timid people, when they became Christians, their inherent character was completely transformed and they always stood firm, bravely refusing to run from persecution.

In the beginning, there were a large number of shamans in Bhabikan's village. All of them, including Bhabikan and his brother, eventually became followers of Jesus. In the last few years, persecution has largely ended and now it has been reported to us that there are perhaps 20,000 believers among the Chepang people.

The LORD is my light and my salvation—
whom shall I fear?
The LORD is the stronghold of my life—
of whom shall I be afraid?
Psalm 27:1

—How the Adventure Began—

(1964-1965)

❧❧

CHAPTER 5

COUNTERFEIT CHRISTIAN

෯෯

Why do you call me, 'Lord, Lord,'
but you do not do what I say?
Luke 6:46

"**G**ary, you don't know what you're talking about!"
Leaping out of her seat, Bonnie slammed my
car door with a bang. Then, never looking back, she
marched up the stairs to her house. What she said was the
truth, and her declaration started me on a pursuit that
turned my life upside down.

It was September 1963 when Bonnie made that claim,
and I can remember it as if it were yesterday. If someone
had asked me if I was a Christian then, I certainly would
have said, "Yes." I believed in God. I believed in Jesus.
After all, I wasn't a Buddhist. I wasn't a Muslim, and I
wasn't a Hindu. I believed in the Bible and went to
church. Well, at least I generally showed up for Christmas
and Easter and never failed to put my dollar bill in the
offering plate.

On the other hand, I knew so little about Christian things that I couldn't even remember what had provoked her so. I had simply repeated something I had learned as a child in Sunday School. And it was this something from the Bible which had upset my girlfriend.

Actually, Bonnie was my fiancée and a confirmed agnostic. She was also an A student at the University of Washington in Seattle, and she was not about to let my fuzzy thinking go unchallenged. I had just been commissioned as an officer in the U.S. Navy, and within the week I was leaving for my ship. She had been so offended by my comment that I thought about it often. As a result, while I was packing to leave a few days later, I asked my mother if I could take the family Bible. The Bible was never read at home, so that was fine with her.

Urged on by Bonnie's rebuke, I began to read the Book. After all, we planned to get married in the coming year, so it seemed only reasonable that I ought to know what I was talking about. Consequently, practically every day I read from both the Old and the New Testaments. In doing so, the more I read, the more questions I had.

It was not apparent to me at first, but I had begun a quest for the truth. Jesus had promised, *you shall know the truth, and the truth will set you free* (John 8:32). In this regard, it seemed obvious that the kind of freedom Jesus was promising would come only if I would earnestly seek the truth. Therefore, I kept on reading and the more I read, the more interested I became.

In January 1964, the ten ships of our amphibious squadron were sent to the Western Pacific on a six-month assignment. That brought us into ports in Japan, Hong Kong, the Philippines and Taiwan. Bonnie and I wrote to one another nearly every day, and while I was in Hong Kong, I bought the special jade wedding ring she wanted. In Japan I also purchased an expensive set of china, as well as the bolts of silk that she requested to make her wedding dress. When our tour was completed in July, our ship returned to home port in San Diego.

Meanwhile, Bonnie had won a scholarship to study at MIT University for the summer. A couple of days after our ship arrived in San Diego, I received a letter from her. It stated that since she had been at MIT, she had come to realize that we weren't suitably matched for each other.

Her letter was a great shock to me. I recognized that she was a superior student, and my accomplishments were not in the academic realm. Nevertheless, I had been looking forward to a lifetime of happiness with her, and I continued to hope that she might change her mind.

As the weeks passed by, I tried to maintain communications with her, and I continued to eagerly read the Bible. In November, I was sent to Communication Officers School. Being away from my ship for six weeks gave me even more time on my own to reflect and read the Bible... sometimes for as much as four hours a day. Alone in my room one Saturday afternoon, I suddenly had a revelation of the depth of my pride, my selfishness, and my willful sin. This led to many tears and a time when I sincerely asked God to forgive me.

Not many days later, I received a letter from Bonnie asking if she could come down to see me at Christmas time in San Diego. I still loved her deeply and felt sure that as soon as I saw her again, I would be captivated by her charm and beauty. I felt that as likely as not, after a couple of days we would go find a Justice of the Peace and get married on the spot.

But what about my search for God? On this point we had been drifting farther and farther apart. On the one hand, I very much wanted to marry her. On the other hand, I could not abandon my search for God. Would this make for a contentious life together? Could our love rise above this difference? I struggled with this predicament for four days, seeking God for an answer.

One afternoon it came to me so clearly, so strongly. No! My search for truth and for God had put too much distance between us. We really were not suitably matched for one another, and that is what I wrote back to her.

About a year earlier, I had been invited to a Christian Servicemen's Center in downtown San Diego. There, for the first time, I had heard and thought I understood the message of the Bible. At the conclusion, we were asked, "Who wants to be saved from hell?" I had never heard a presentation like this before, and I raised my hand along with several others. Afterwards, we were herded into a little room where we were led through a joint prayer and asked to sign a card.

What I remember about that short time was that we had prayed the "Sinner's Prayer." Therefore, we were told, this meant we were saved from hell and now had a place reserved in heaven. This was certain, so we should never let anyone put doubt in our minds about it! It all sounded okay to me. In any event, I thought, when judgment day came, it was good to have this "sinner's prayer" thing as a trump card.

I, however, had only superficially gone through some Christian formalities. With my lips and in my mind I had "accepted" Jesus. I had "received" Jesus. I had made an intellectual assent to the fact that He was the Savior of the world. I had done the "right" thing, and prayed the "right" words, but nothing had truly changed in my heart. Now, I figured, I had acquired my fire-escape for the Day of Judgment. In fact, I was a *counterfeit* Christian.

In the following months, I tried to be better and began going to church more often. I drank less and was careful not to blaspheme or curse quite so often, but my life goals continued to be fixed on self-fulfillment and pleasure.

I really did try to do what I thought a good Christian should do. In fact, while our ship was in Japan, I had regularly gone to Christian meetings. There, on two occasions I had been asked when it was that I had become a believer. To that, I had confidently cited the day I had prayed the Sinner's Prayer.

January 2, 1965 found me at a conference center in the San Bernardino Mountains of Southern California. I had been invited by students attending College Avenue Baptist Church in San Diego. That evening, I asked my friend Randy about something I hadn't understood. He took me back to my bunk and showed me some Scriptures. What particularly caught my attention was Jesus' promise in John 10:10 that He had come to give me life *more* abundantly.

My father was a moderately successful businessman. He owned a small yacht which we took around the islands of Puget Sound and fished from at every opportunity. He also had six horses that we rode into the remote high country of the Cascade Mountains where we camped, fished, and hunted. After my stint in the Navy, I knew that he would be delighted to have me come back to work alongside him. Consequently, I felt I had opportunities to prosper and that a rather good life was already laid out ahead of me. Nonetheless, I couldn't stop thinking about God's promise of "more." I reasoned that if God was God, then He certainly was able to do what He said.

By now I had absorbed enough of the Bible to realize that Jesus was both the Lord and Savior... not just one or the other. If I refused to make Jesus truly the Lord of my life, could I expect Him to still be my Savior? Would He save me from myself if I wasn't prepared to make Him my Lord? It seemed doubtful to me.

Additionally, I somehow calculated that if I did not earnestly and truthfully follow His guidance, I could not expect Him to give me the "more" abundant life. Maybe it was because of my degree in Business, but anyhow I decided I would make a contract with God. In my heart I promised to do what He wanted me to do, go where He wanted me to go, and say what He wanted me to say. I only needed to be certain that it was Him who was directing my path... not some church, not someone's favorite creed, nor some charismatic preacher. God's part of the agreement was that He would lead me into a life that was more abundant... wherever and whatever that might be.

For me, this event was completely unemotional. Nevertheless, it was a decision and commitment I made with my whole heart and soul. Henceforth, to the best of my ability, I would obey Jesus and He would be the Lord of my life.

About a day later I began to notice that the worry and anxiety in my life had faded away. Amazingly, this was being replaced by a steadily increasing joy and peace far beyond anything I had ever experienced before. Within a few days, it became perfectly clear that indeed, God had invaded my life. As He had promised, Jesus had come to dwell within me. He had become my Friend. Now I began to hear the Holy Spirit speaking in my heart so wonderfully and sometimes so clearly. Fear of death and fear of judgment had fled away, and I had been born anew into the Kingdom of God.

But when He, the Spirit of truth, comes,
He will guide you into all truth.
John 16:13

—Postscript—

In retrospect, there was no significant difference between the prayers I spoke on January 2nd and those I had voiced some thirteen months earlier. On the first occasion, I simply repeated what I had been told to say. I thought that this would provide me with an escape from hell, and henceforth, I tried to be a little better. I had become a pseudo-Christian. I believed in Jesus, but only in my head and with my lips. I would follow and be obedient to Him just as long as it didn't interfere with my own plans for a prosperous and pleasure-filled life.

But in putting my own desires first, I had never considered *God's desires* and *God's plan*. I had not realized that God is bent on creating a family for Himself... those who in Christ have learned to conquer the lusts of the flesh and the pride of life. He wants children who in Jesus' power have battled Satan and assaulted the gates of hell. He is looking for sons and daughters who will walk and talk with Him as a friend. He desires people who are filled with His compassion and who love the unlovely… those who are being prepared to do great things throughout eternity.

When I had repented so fervently about eleven months later, I had only agreed with God's assessment of my selfish, sinful life. And though I was beginning to call out to God and sometimes even listen for answers from Him, I certainly had not given Him my heart and life. At best, my repentance was only partial. Chiefly, I just wanted to be good enough to escape hell-fire. On Judgment Day, I simply wanted to be really certain that my good deeds would pile up higher on the scales of justice than my bad ones.

This second time I prayed, however, my prayer included the component of my heart. While outwardly the words were nearly the same, inwardly my heart was silently speaking to God a prayer of total commitment. It was then that I had asked Jesus to truly be King of my life. No longer would my life be seeking fulfillment in pleasure and prosperity. Now my focus would be on building the Kingdom of Heaven, rather than on myself. It was this desire that opened the door of my heart to the Holy Spirit.

As for Bonnie, I still loved her very much. However, this encounter with God created an ever-widening chasm between us. I ardently hoped that she would begin a search for God as I had and that we still might have a wonderful life together. But it was not to be.

I saw her one more time, a year-and-a-half later. Soon thereafter I lost track of her, only hearing that she had gone to Taiwan to teach school and that she had married another school teacher there. Over the years, I often prayed for this lovely young lady who captured my heart and had goaded me to find the truth. That truth brought me great joy and peace in Jesus Christ, and I fervently hoped that one day she too would find the same.

Jesus answered, 'I am the way,
the truth and the life.'
John 14:6

USS Catamount (LSD-17)

CHAPTER 6

THE SECRET INVASION

১৯৯

Secretly, our warship steamed across the Pacific Ocean. We were ready for battle… loaded with marines and all their weaponry. Our target was Hanoi, and I was to lead the first wave in!

Towards the end of WW II, the USS Catamount (LSD-17) participated in attacks against Japan and later in the Korean War. During an amphibious assault, our ship was one of four in our squadron designated to take responsibility for a beachhead. Out at sea, I was to organize the landing craft into groups, and lead the first wave in to the beach. Just before hitting land, I was to turn off to one side.

The landing craft would drop their marines, reverse off the beach, and return to sea to pick up another load from our troop ships. Winds and tides could be unpredictable, and landing craft could get broached, disabled or stranded. It was my duty to manage the beach and to get the troops ashore as quickly as possible.

When I came aboard ship as a new Ensign in 1963, I was told that I could get excused from a boring routine on the ship... if I volunteered for a special assignment. I had grown up on Whidbey Island in Puget Sound, and riding in small boats was second nature to me. I couldn't have been happier than with a boat bucking beneath my feet, and the wind and sea spray in my face. This assignment could be pure hell for someone who got seasick, but it would just be another fun adventure for me.

Now it was February 1965, and the war in Vietnam was beginning to ramp up. Our squadron of ten ships had sailed out to Hawaii to participate in our annual War Games training event. A month earlier I had become the new Communications Officer for our ship, but there hadn't been time to train up a new Ensign to lead an amphibious assault. Just before the training exercise had begun, we received unexpected orders to steam at top speed for Pearl Harbor. As darkness fell, our squadron silently made its way into Pearl to find the docks already filling with marines and their equipment. All night, all day, and all the next night our ships loaded, and the following morning we quietly slipped out to sea.

Electronic communication was strictly prohibited, and in those days before satellites, it was as if we had disappeared off the edge of the earth. Between ships, communication was by Morse code using our spotlights or with our flags. Each day we received new orders from Pearl, "Proceed to point X in the ocean." Drawing a line through the Xs put us right into Hanoi! Pearl Harbor continued to send us coded messages over the airwaves, but every ship remained totally silent as we stealthily made our way across the Pacific.

An amphibious landing

Storming the beach

It had all started so innocently, and I had not counted on this. Now it would be the real deal with real bullets! Spending all day going around in little circles off a Hanoi beach while wave after wave of landing craft came and went would be so obvious. The enemy would quickly realize that I was the one managing the beach... and surely I would become a priority target.

Two weeks later as we cruised through the waters off Hanoi, we received orders to turn north and off-load our marines on Okinawa, Japan. President Johnson had been prevailed upon to change his mind. Instead of cutting off the Russian supply ships that were pouring into Hanoi Harbor and stopping the North Vietnamese troops that were streaming south, he would put our soldiers into the jungles of South Vietnam and fight them there. We would never learn why.

—Postscript—

At the time, President Johnson did not know that he had just doomed 58,000 American men and countless allies to die in those ghastly jungles. He did not know that ruthless regimes would take over Cambodia, Laos, and South Vietnam, and slaughter not just thousands, but millions and millions of innocent civilians. If he had glimpsed even a small inkling of the human cost of his decision, what would have been my fate? I suppose that I would have led the first wave in.

As for me, just six weeks earlier on January 2nd, there had been another invasion... this one also unseen. Once again I had made a decision to volunteer. In response, God had given an order for His Spirit to establish a beachhead in my heart, and Jesus Christ was managing it all.

I was transported from the sea of death, and He had set my feet on the shores of life. The assault was victorious, and a worry-plagued soul was conquered by a peace that thoroughly amazed me... and was I glad! For the first time in my life, I really trusted God with all my heart and I had *learned to be content whatever the circumstances* (Philippians 4:11).

Never before had I known the expectation of real danger without fear and oppressive worry. It all seemed so impossible. As our warship closed in on Hanoi, no anxiety could be found in my heart or mind. None! Every night I slept soundly and awoke refreshed. God's Word was true... *the peace of God, which transcends all understanding, will guard your hearts and your minds in Christ Jesus* (Philippians 4:7).

I had begun to live by the Word, and its power was plainly evident. Fear of death and judgment had fled from the presence of Jesus. The Spirit of God had secreted His promises into my heart, and the invasion was successful. All glory to His Name!

The LORD will keep you from all harm —
He will watch over your life;
The LORD will watch over your
coming and going
both now and forevermore.
Psalm 121:7-8

CHAPTER 7

THE DOVES

∂∞∂

Delight yourself in the LORD and
He will give you the desires of your heart.
Psalm 37:4

When I was growing up, real life for we three Shepherd boys was filled with boating, skiing, hunting, fishing, horseback riding and most any sport… anything that was outdoors. In our little rural town of Oak Harbor, many people were deeply religious. That meant that Sunday was a particularly good day for us to go hunting and fishing since the competition was greatly reduced.

On January 2, 1965, while I was debating whether to give my life to God or not, my biggest concern was to what degree His demands would interfere with my enjoying an exciting and fulfilling life. Somehow I had assumed that God would make me become a Pastor, and I couldn't imagine anything more boring. Furthermore, Pastors had to work on Sunday, so that was one less day for me to go hunting or fishing. Nevertheless, God held out to me Jesus' promise that He had come to give me life more abundantly (John 10:10).

With that verse, God reassured me and encouraged me not to be concerned about hunting and fishing. As long as I chose to follow His plan, it would be His responsibility to ensure that my life would be more fulfilling. In the end, I simply trusted His promise that night.

As for us, one of our family traditions was to travel to Wenatchee in Eastern Washington for the opening day of dove hunting season on the 1st of September. At that time, there would be thousands upon thousands of birds swarming in and out of the harvested wheat fields. Mother had a delicious recipe for cooking doves with mushroom soup over rice, and we always looked forward to those special meals.

The bag limit was ten birds per day. Nevertheless, it was surprisingly difficult to hit the doves as they jetted up and down the windy ravines. The result was that we shot and shot and shot in our attempts to bag our limit of doves. Sometimes we would compete with one another to see who could get ten birds with the least number of shells. Expending just two boxes of shells, fifty shots, was considered very good shooting. Eight or ten shots per bird was more the average. One year, on the third day of the hunt, I had my all-time best shooting record when I bagged ten birds with exactly twenty-five shots.

A few years later, I was stationed on a Navy ship in San Diego, and it was at this time that I gave my life over to God. When I didn't have duty aboard ship, I would try to attend two different churches in the morning. However, after I met my future wife, Barbara, I discovered that her church in nearby El Cajon was much to my liking, and I eagerly joined in with all their programs.

LTJG Gary Shepherd

In 1965, September 1st fell on a Saturday. As usual, I went to the men's Saturday morning prayer meeting. On that early morning, Pastor Graham and the head elder, Bevin Walker, were the only ones to show up. Bevin had a dairy farm in nearby Santee, and when we were finished he told me to come out and hunt doves on his land. I declined. I hadn't hunted in nearly two years, nor did I have my shotgun. Bevin continued to insist that I come and offered me the use of his shotgun.

Bevin's gun was a heavy, long-barreled 12 gauge, not at all suited for shooting fast-moving doves. Later that morning when I got out to his stock pond, I found his sons sitting amid a great number of empty shells along with the few birds they had bagged. They suggested that I go over and sit next to a nearby fence post. Soon, high in the air a dove came streaking past. To their astonishment, my shot dropped the bird. After picking it up, another dove came over, high and fast. I dropped it also!

Then, for a while there were no more birds. I could see now that there wouldn't be much more action around the pond that morning, so I left them and wandered off into the nearby floodplain of the dried-up San Diego River. There, the birds burst out of trees, came rocketing by from one side or the other, or suddenly appeared from behind. It was every sort of shot to test a hunter.

The limit by then had been increased to twelve birds. I didn't have my trained retriever, so I couldn't locate two birds that fell into thick brush. Nevertheless, thirty minutes later I returned to the stock pond with my limit of twelve. I had fired eighteen shells and only four shots had been misses!

—Postscript—

On Whidbey Island, hunting was so much a part of life that at one time, the public schools used to be given a holiday on the first day of bird season. That allowed the students and teachers to freely hunt without having to skip classes.

It would be many years before I had another opportunity to hunt doves, and never again would I shoot in such an accurate way. But it didn't matter. God had promised to give me life more abundantly. In a surprising manner that was unique to me, He had demonstrated that He was able and willing to do just that. This experience greatly encouraged me to follow Him in high faith, no matter where that path took me.

—Episodes from Baju's Life—

(1973-1996)

CHAPTER 8

THAT CONFIDENCE

‿◦❧

When you go through deep waters and great trouble,
I will be with you.
Isaiah 43:2

How could he not be confident in every trial? The Son had gladly taken the rightful punishment for this sinner of sinners, and he, Baju, had been invited with open arms into the Father's house. Such was the Man that was at his side.

Other than finding a New Testament for Baju to read in 1973, it seemed that we had little to do with the remarkable changes in his life. From the time that he committed himself to following Jesus, he faced strong opposition. When he steadfastly refused to take part in the village sacrifices, he was ridiculed and then threatened. He was considered a trouble-maker, a rebel. After all, he no longer acclaimed the King of Nepal as the incarnation of the Hindu god, Vishnu. The police were summoned.

This was nothing strange for Baju. Before he became a follower of Jesus, he was a village pest. He had a reputation for paying people who worked his fields less than their full wages. And when he purchased meat or something else in the village, he would sometimes give only a partial payment. When they asked for the remaining amount later on, he would become angry and start a fight. In addition to his hard drinking and carousing, he had been a constant pain in the neck to almost everyone. In short, he was regularly disrupting the important harmony of village life.

So, some fifteen years earlier, Baju had been given the village's most severe punishment. The rogue was "thrown out" of the village. Actually, I have been unable to find an English term comparable to the Magar word *bahit*. It does not mean that he was physically driven out of his village. Rather, it means he was shunned and made an outcast.

His sentence was for a full 365 days. During that time he and his family were to be treated as if they were lower than the lowest of the untouchable castes. No one was allowed to come into his house and he was not allowed to go into anyone else's. He was ostracized and most of all, heaped with great shame.

Shame, a continuous, daily shame for 52 weeks! Furthermore, no one in his family was allowed to use the nearby water sources, which made a difficult life even harder. If disaster struck or a storm was to take the roof off his house, it was his tough luck... no villager was allowed to help or assist him in any way. When his sentence was completed, they assumed that he had learned his lesson and he was restored. On that day all restrictions were removed.

Now, with this new development in his life, would they shun or expel him once again? The shame on Baju would be intolerable... to most people, at least. Baju, however, would not wear the shame. Physically, he had already suffered much more than his fellow villagers.

As a Gurkha soldier in the British Army, his unit had been sent to the Afghanistan border to fight the ancestors of the modern-day Taliban. In 1937, he was leading his patrol up a dry streambed when he stepped on a mine. The blast shattered his arm and his foot was blown off. At the British military hospital in Abbottabad, the first operation removed the remnants of his leg below the knee. (Abbottabad is the same city where 74 years later the terrorist, Osama Bin Laden, was found.) Then, a second operation was required above his knee. The gangrene, however, could not be stopped and a third operation took his leg off at the hip.

As he lay in that hospital week after week and month after month, all he wanted was to die. For an extended time, he even refused to eat, but still he didn't die. Meanwhile, his British officer did everything possible to see that his life was saved, and providentially it was.

Now, some thirty-five years later, Baju learned that in ancient times God had walked and talked with mankind's forefather, Adam. That, he understood, is obviously what his Heavenly Father ever so much desired to restore... right now... with Baju. It was the companionship, or as King Solomon put it, *a friend who sticks closer than a brother* (Proverbs 18:24). Why else would the Man who called him "friend" have suffered so much?

Consequently, though his allegiance to Jesus caused Baju to suffer often and much, nothing seemed to shake his confidence. Even if none understood him, even though everyone forsook him, he understood "The Plan." After all, it was simply the age-old power struggle between God and Satan.

Before mankind was formed, Satan thought that he would have a turn at being God and decided to ascend to the throne. However, it didn't work out. Instead, a cosmic war erupted and he and his supporting angels were cast out of heaven (Isaiah 14:13-15). Now, the only thing they had on their wicked minds was revenge. Since they were unable to overcome God himself, the next best thing was to wreak havoc on His family, on those who were created in His image.

Yes, it was a power struggle. Of course the battle was completely unfair… flesh-encumbered, easily-deceived humans pitted against powerful, unseen spirit-beings. But God had a plan… a plan to defeat and humiliate those proud spirits. He would use Jesus living in weak and puny human beings to triumph over the devil in the name of Jesus.

God's sons and daughters would suffer greatly… that Baju understood… that Baju expected. Even though that victory might not be seen immediately, those who chose Him as their indwelling friend would overcome Lucifer. They would penetrate the Kingdom of Darkness and bring Light to the hearts of many. They would wrest captives from the hands of the Evil One. They would order those spirits to go to the bottomless pit or to the feet of Jesus… and the power in that Name would compel them to do so (Psalm 110:1).

Why else did the Book proclaim that *God has not given us a spirit of fear; but of power, and of love, and of a sound/disciplined mind* (2 Timothy 1:7).

Yes, Baju would not fear the shame. He would not wear it. He would keep the same mind as did Jesus. *When they hurled their insults at Him, He did not retaliate; when He suffered, He made no threats* (1 Peter 2:23).

That shame was false, a concoction made up by Satan and those whom he had deceived. Furthermore, King David had declared, *No one whose hope is in You will ever be put to shame* (Psalm 25:3). That is how God saw it, and that was okay with Baju. God, on the other hand, had given him power... unadulterated divine power. It was a power to be controlled by love and a disciplined mind. It was a power to love the most loveless, and to maintain a disciplined life that could courageously face every trial.

Though Baju was never brought before the village council for abandoning the village sacrifices, nevertheless he left his house in Arakhala and crossed the gorge to live in his out-of-the-way hut up on Peak-of-the-gods. There, he could draw water from his own spring in the forest, and look after the few fields that he owned up there.

In the meantime, he would pray. He would pray, confident of the impending victory. He would walk and talk with God and pray, and pray, and pray. He was confident that his Father would answer those prayers... those desires that echoed in his Father's heart. "Lord, build your church here! Build it right here!"

But God never did.

Instead, for seventeen years Baju was the only follower of Jesus in Arakhala Village. Even when Adina and Michael's village friends grew up and in 1990 began, one or two at a time to join with him, still there was continued persecution and harassment. Nevertheless, Baju remained confident to the very end. When his earthly journey ended in November 1996, there were only eight young men that still stood by him. In fact, his only son succumbed to the village ways and insisted that the Hindu rituals be performed on Baju's mortal body.

—Postscript—

Though Baju never saw his prayers answered, he remained confident. He had no doubt that God's plan would prevail. He realized that there was much he did not understand. In particular, I remember him wondering out loud how God could be so slow. But not seeing and not understanding were never satisfactory reasons to weaken his confidence in the Father. All men may be liars, but his God would prove Himself true. One day, his Father would do it! Of that, he died certain.

Now, thirty-six years after Baju began to follow Jesus, and seventeen years after the first young men joined him, there have been some significant changes. From the portals of heaven, Baju has been watching it unfold.

We ourselves saw very little until 2007. At that time, Baju's grandson, Mailha, was working overseas in Malaysia when his wife, Tema, was overcome by demons. The demons often bragged that they would devour her, and indeed over the next six months her body withered away until she was just skin and bones. The family offered many blood sacrifices and tried all of their ancient ways to help. But when her shaman grandfather could do no more, he sent her to the Christians in Arakhala who prayed for her and she was delivered.

She had been drawing water from that same spring in the forest, and working in those same fields on Peak-of-the-gods. After her deliverance, she asked permission from Baju's son to hold some simple meetings with a few lady friends from Arakhala. We were surprised when he consented. He knew, however, that her life clearly had been saved by the prayers of the Christians.

In 2009, Baju's grandson returned home from working in Malaysia. He knew that he was fortunate to still have a wife and soon after, he too became a follower of Jesus. By 2010, within one short year, out of the 125 people who live on Peak-of-the-gods, about 35 have begun to follow Jesus. Indeed, God had done a work of power because of Baju's love and disciplined life. On the very spot where Baju had prayed, God has built His church!

But if you suffer for doing good and you endure it,
this is commendable before God.
To this you were called, because
Christ suffered for you, leaving you an
example, that you should follow in His steps.
1 Peter 2:20-21

CHAPTER 9

SATAN ON TRIAL

༈

The god of this world has blinded the minds
of them which believe not.
2 Corinthians 4:4

There was no defense to be made. The accused was clearly guilty. For all intents and purposes, the trial was over before it had begun. Really, the only thing to be decided was the appropriate penalty.

The punishment in Magar society, however, was minor compared to the shame. The greatest penalty would be that stigma… the shame the guilty party and his family would forever bear.

When an accusation is made, Magar custom requires an immediate resolution, even if it takes the whole night. Sitting in a loose circle, a representative from every household listened carefully. The proceedings began with Baju's accusation, "Shami's son is a thief!"

This was nothing new… her son was well known for stealing. However, he had never been brought to trial. No one had the courage to do that. No one was foolish enough. This time, however, he had stolen a new shirt from Baju's door-less hut up on Peak-of-the-gods. When Baju realized that his shirt had disappeared, Shami's son was the first one he suspected. The following day, Baju went down to their tiny house, and found no one at home. In those days, there were no doors on the huts up there, so he went inside and with little effort found his shirt hidden away beneath a few belongings.

Any sane person would have left the matter right there. Indeed, it took a very daring, if not dim-witted person to have even searched Shami's dwelling. She was a witch with powerful *mechonda*... familiar spirits, which did her bidding. For sure, no one wanted to make her mad!

So, this trial was supposed to be about stealing. And though Shami's son was judged guilty, this really was not about stealing at all. It wasn't even about right or wrong. At the heart of it, this wasn't about forgiveness or retribution either.

Instead, it was all about the Kingdom of Darkness. That was what was on trial. The Light had freed Baju from its grasp. Now, like one of the old prophets from ancient times, even though there was not a single villager who dared to publicly support him, he was not backing down from this confrontation.

Jesus proved that He had authority to forgive sins by the miracles he performed (Matthew 9:6). Similarly, by casting out the most powerful of demons, He had proven His authority over the Kingdom of Darkness (Mark 5:8). When Baju responded to Jesus' invitation, it was not just to become a servant or disciple, but also to be a special brother and beloved friend (John 15:15). Like the Christians 2,000 years earlier, he knew that this authority was also his (Mark 16:15-17). As a result, he slept every night in complete peace.

I wish I had known that this trial was taking place that night. I would have loved to have gone and sat outside the circle to listen. And how I would have liked to have been able to read the minds of the villagers sitting there!

Surely they would have been astounded that Baju dared to confront those evil powers. Not a few would have had trembling hearts, fearful that Shami would loose her spirits upon them. Now, more than ever before, Baju would be the target of Shami and her *mechonda*. Just as likely, every other witch around might join in and attack him. If there was any good news here, it was that as long as the witches were preoccupied with Baju, perhaps they might neglect the rest of them.

A year later, however, Baju was healthier and happier than ever. Now, of course, it would seem that the village citizens would be eagerly seeking to acquire the same power that protected him. Wrong! That was not the case at all.

For another ten years, Baju remained the sole follower of Jesus in Arakhala. For uncounted centuries, the Powers of Darkness had held these people and their ancestors securely in their grip. Fear, and particularly fear of death, was their chief weapon. The icy grip of fear kept the villagers blinded from comprehending or seeing the light of the Son of God.

When I chatted with the villagers in those days, it was not unusual for them to talk about Baju. Often they would exclaim, "When the witch eats our blood, we become sick and get thinner and thinner. Baju, however, just gets fatter and fatter!"

That certainly was the case. When we first came to Arakhala, Baju looked just like all the rest of the people... thin and undernourished. But by now, Baju had become the fattest man in the village.

—Postscript—

This trial was a watershed moment. The Kingdom of God had begun its move. In clear and no uncertain terms, the Kingdom of Darkness was put on notice. Its very gates were now under attack. An old soldier, a sinner of sinners had been recruited, and he was actively looking to take territory for his King and Prince. As Jesus had solemnly predicted:

> *On this rock I will build my church,*
> *and the gates of hell will not overcome it.*
> Matthew 16:18

CHAPTER 10

RIGHTEOUSNESS, PEACE AND JOY

ॐ

*He saved us, not because of the righteous things
we had done, but because of His mercy.*
Titus 3:5

B aju grew up in a world where shamans and witchdoctors wielded great power. Their religion was one of animism mixed with Hindu thought, whose teachers were shamans, Brahman pundits, and mystic yogis. The deep jungle and the darkness in particular, were filled with dreaded spirits and demons. Above all, apprehension of evil omens and the fear of death ruled over village life.

For Baju, however, this all changed when at the age of 61, he began reading the Nepali New Testament and asked Jesus to become the Lord of his life. Baju promptly went from being a scoundrel and reprobate to become a person who followed God more clearly and consistently than anyone I have ever known. Yet, at the same time, some of his Bible interpretations were clearly off base. For some while, I used to be puzzled how Baju could hold an incorrect understanding of some Scriptures and yet walk so closely with God.

Two reasons he walked so closely come to mind: Jesus taught that the person who is forgiven most, loves the most (Luke 7:36-50). More than once, Baju confided in me that he had committed every sin in the Book. And just as Jesus had predicted, when he learned that God's forgiveness had no limits, his gratefulness knew no bounds. This overflowing love for God energized him then to share his discovery with others.

Secondly, when he put his trust in God, he found his forgiveness was in Jesus Christ. "In" is a key to understanding Baju's life. He came to realize that while he stayed in Christ, he obtained the same rights and privileges as Jesus. And in "putting on Christ," he understood that when God looked at him, He saw His Son Jesus. Though he himself, from time to time would recall his sins, God said He remembered them no more (Hebrews 8:12). That was incredibly good news. And since God didn't remember them, he was certain that he stood righteous in God's presence.

In this manner, Baju fully grasped the truth that no amount of good works on his part was ever going to offset his great and many sins. And like Abraham, he learned that trusting God was the only way that righteousness could be obtained (Romans 4). Trust was what Baju always did. Specifically, he trusted that Jesus' blood washed his sins away. Like King David, he could confidently say, *No one will be condemned who takes refuge in Him* (Psalm 34:22).

As such, he never seemed to consider saying "No" to God. Consequently, the increasingly close fellowship he experienced with Jesus prompted him to trust God all the more.

Because he could not be moved off that foundation of righteousness, I never knew Baju to be fearful. As for worry, it might catch him occasionally, but only for a moment. And, because his heart and mind remained "in" Christ, he constantly enjoyed the fruit of righteousness, which is the peace of Jesus, a *peace which transcends all understanding* (Philippians 4:7).

Living in Christ and in His peace gave Baju joy... a joy that was pervasive and contagious. Every day was a good day. Every day was a happy day, and his face and demeanor clearly showed it. And why not? Jesus was Baju's friend, and the Holy Spirit was his constant companion (John 15:14).

Personally, I have found Baju's example to be a helpful way to measure how closely I myself am walking with Jesus. Like a train's engine, righteousness puts into motion everything that follows. As my trust level in God increases, the effective power of that righteousness also increases. Furthermore, a powerful peace follows right behind this trust-righteousness. And right behind the peace rolls joy... a joy stirred by the presence of the Holy Spirit.

The opposite is also true. When I have a fickle trust, it undermines the closeness I have with Jesus. Thus, in difficult times that powerful peace is missing. And that results in a lack of joy and experiencing even less of the Holy Spirit's presence and power.

*For the kingdom of God is… righteousness,
peace and joy in the Holy Spirit.*
Romans 14:17

Adina's birthday in the village

CHAPTER 11

THE DEADLY TRAIL
ॐ∞ॐ

H er decision was fatal!

Running for home through the storm, she stepped on a wet, flat rock. The next day their bodies were discovered by the villagers of Chuli Bojha. She and her young son had slipped over the side of the narrow trail and plummeted to the rocks below.

At this very spot, Baju too, had gone over the side during the monsoon season some years earlier. Against all odds, however, he lived to tell the tale.

That day, Baju had left his home to travel to Kathmandu. He was to live with us there, and work with me for a couple of months. Rain was falling gently that morning, and he was all alone as he toiled up the trail towards the pass. Then without warning, he suddenly flew over the side.

In these rugged mountains, the trails scratched out of the steep hillsides are sometimes wide enough for scarcely one person. If you are fortunate when your foot slips, either there are some bushes or trees for you to grab onto, or else the mountainside is not exceedingly steep. However, in most places there are no trees below the trail, and there is nothing to stop you from tumbling to the bottom, fifty feet, a hundred feet, or in some places a thousand feet or more below. More often than not, it felt to me that the sides of these trails had death written all over them.

For Baju, it was a worst case scenario. The rising mountain ridge was on his right, and the chasm, the side on which he had no leg, was on his left. At this point, he was pushing hard on his crutches to make the ascent to the pass. When his left crutch slipped on the wet rock, the other crutch, coupled with the momentum of his push, propelled him sideways into empty space. That is all he could remember.

Miraculously, Baju found himself about eight feet down. He was balanced there on the nearly vertical mountainside, one hand holding on to a small bush. After he had reoriented himself, he used the protruding rocks and thick tufts of hardy grass to pull himself back up onto the trail.

Many, if not most, would have taken this as an omen of impending doom. They would have turned around and immediately headed back home. But seemingly unruffled by this minor delay, Baju gathered up his crutches and continued on toward the pass. This brave old soldier had a job to do. It was to turn the Word of God into his heart language, into the language of his Magar people.

When Baju finally reached Kathmandu a day and a half later, he had unraveled the mystery of how it had all happened. When I opened our front door, he launched straightaway into his story, "God's angels have saved me!"

Before he traveled anywhere, Baju never failed to ask God to send His angels to protect and assist him on the journey. This experience, he was certain, was a time when God had done exactly that.

For He will command His angels concerning you
to guard you in all your ways.
They will lift you up in their hands.
Psalm 91:11-12

—Postscript—

It would have been an incalculable loss for us if Baju had been seriously hurt or killed at this time. We were finally making good progress on analyzing the complex intricacies of Magar grammar and translating the New Testament. He was highly skilled at manipulating the Magar language, and he was learning to make his mother tongue clearly and smoothly express the complicated writings of Paul.

This incident occurred nine years before there were any other believers in Arakhala Village. Had he been killed in this manner, it would surely have been interpreted as the impotence of his God to protect him from the malicious spirits and witches' curses. Who, then, would have found the courage to follow Jesus, if he had died like this?

A rest stop on the trail

CHAPTER 12

BAJU'S GIFTS

෯෨

Forgive us our sins, for we also
forgive everyone who sins against us.
Luke 11:4

I t was an annual event and it always bothered me.
Sometimes it really irritated me.

Once a year, Baju would go out to the town of
Bharatpur to collect his army pension. Historically, the
disbursement office had been down in India and it was so
far away and difficult to reach that the retired soldiers
would make the two-week trek to collect their pensions
only once a year. So even when a closer office was
opened and they could reach it within two days, most of
them continued to collect their pensions just once
annually.

Some years it seemed worse to me than others, and
eventually I didn't bother to ask him about it. He didn't
seem to be making good choices and at best, it was a very
poor investment. But in time, I learned that there was no

way I was going to persuade him otherwise. I knew what he would say.

God had made the choice first. He had chosen to forgive Baju, and lift the crushing mountain of sin from off his shoulders. Secondly, Baju had chosen to accept that offer and seal it by totally repenting and asking God to forgive him. He had asked God to include him in that great congregation that through the ages was covered by the blood of Jesus' sacrifice. And thirdly, Baju was exceedingly grateful to God. Consequently, he was determined to follow God's word and imitate His Son Jesus as closely as he could… and one of those things that Jesus had taught was, *Give to everyone who asks you* (Luke 6:30).

For the most part, Baju took that quite literally. Upon returning to Arakhala with his yearly pension, he would be besieged by distant relatives and dubious friends, all of whom had "critical" needs. To be polite, of course, they would only ask him for a loan. But short of a miracle, there was no way that most of those destitute people were going to find enough to repay their loan. Furthermore, he knew it.

Baju had more land and better fields on those mountains than the average family. And, most importantly, in years when the leopards were not particularly bad, he had twenty-five or more cattle that he herded in the jungle. They provided that all-important manure which was so necessary to produce a crop in the thin rocky soil. Even so, he never could grow enough corn to feed his small family for twelve months. So he, too, still had to purchase rice from the Brahmins down in the valley.

Upon receiving his pension in Bharatpur, he would buy his wife, Kissery, one blouse and one skirt... the village's customary annual allotment for clothing. Then he would purchase a set of clothes for the two orphans they were raising, as well as something for himself. He would buy some sulfur and salt peter to manufacture home-made gun powder for his muzzle-loader. And finally, he might get a few pounds of sugar, some cheap tea and peppercorns, as well as a bit of kerosene. Then he would set aside some money to purchase salt and the rice they would need for the rest of the year. The remainder he proceeded to give away!

I don't think I ever quite got over it. I knew the doubtful character of some of those to whom he would loan 10,000 or even 15,000 rupees. Can you imagine yourself loaning $15,000 to some shady character in town, knowing that it would be incredible if he returned even ten percent of it? But Baju did. Furthermore, he did it year after year.

It seemed that he couldn't help himself. They asked, so he gave, and gave, and gave... until after two or three days his yearly pension had vanished. And, just as God had done for him, he did not give according to a person's past record.

Because God had a free will, He could forgive and forget one's past, if He so desired. And because God desired to reestablish a meaningful relationship with mankind, this is what He did. If God did it, then Baju wanted to do it. And because God did not judge Baju's sins, as he so abundantly deserved, Baju, too, did not judge others. Since he refused to stand in judgment on others, he was free from the debilitating emotions that capture those who won't forgive.

Intuitively, Baju seemed to understand that as a human being, God had given him three choices: He could judge, he could forgive, or he could capitulate.

For nearly 50 years, alcohol had been the bane of his life, and his friends and cronies were constantly badgering him to drink with them once again. So, the easy way would have been to eventually give in.

Alternatively, he could judge his friends and remind them what evil, irresponsible people they were. But by judging them, his mind would just as surely be captured by the alcohol… only just in another manner. Alcohol would control his thought life every time he saw someone drinking. Though it didn't control his body, the alcohol would just as certainly maintain control of his mind and emotions with thoughts that judged others. That would produce a simmering anger and resentment that would constantly eat away at his soul.

The only way to be free from this dilemma was to forgive. Forgiveness didn't make it right. However, that was not the point at all. Forgiveness sets us free, just as it sets the other person free. They can continue on in the same way, yet their behavior does not control our minds or our emotions, and we can still care about them and love them. Forgiveness has nothing to do with agreeing with their actions or saying that what they do is right. It has to do with giving the first place to God's gift of a free will. That is real love in action.

Baju's Gifts

But love your enemies, do good to them, and lend to
them without expecting to get anything back.
Then your reward will be great and you will be sons of
the Most High, because He is kind
to the ungrateful and wicked.
Luke 6:35

Michael and Adina carrying mangos home

CHAPTER 13

GOOD NEWS IN TIBET

శ్రీ

And by faith (Abel) still speaks,
even though he is dead.
Hebrews 11:4

Dorci was a prisoner of the Chinese Communists. He had been arrested in Tibet, and now he could rot in jail for the rest of his life. Here, he had no one to call upon for help.

We had known Dorci as a young language helper. He was from the Lhomi tribe, a small Tibetan group that straddles the China-Nepal border east of Mt. Everest. In the early 1970s, a number of us were working on different languages, and during the monsoon season, we would bring our language helpers into Kathmandu to work with us. In the evenings and on weekends, some of them would get together for fellowship or to share a meal. Among them, our Baju was the oldest.

Over those weeks and months together, Dorci listened closely to the experiences Baju would share. As the only follower of Jesus in Arakhala Village, Baju had endured continuous persecution. He had escaped from beatings. He had been jailed and brought before the governor. He had slipped, and gone over the side of a cliff. Then, there were the many healing miracles and much, much more.

Dorci himself was one of the younger language helpers, and a shy person. If there were more than five or six people around, he could hardly make a peep. However, if there were just three or four others he could be very bold when it came to sharing about his hope in Jesus. When he was back in his village, Dorci often took it upon himself to reach out to his fellow Lhomis who lived upriver north of the border.

So, many years later, when Dorci crossed the border into Tibet to do business, he aroused no suspicion. Tibetans are well-known as traders, and they regularly carry products out from the Himalayas to trade down in the lowlands. There, they acquire goods from the south to trade in the north. While he was in that border village, he took every opportunity to share the Good News... and Baju's experiences were his favorite examples. So, although Baju was called away to heaven in 1996, to this day he still speaks... in a Tibetan tribal language.

On one occasion, not many years ago, Dorci was arrested in that Tibetan village. Being reprimanded or interrogated by the police is one thing, but being arrested is another. When he was brought before the local authorities, they decided to send him to the Administrative Center five days' journey upriver. And because of the seriousness of the charges, four policemen continuously guarded him.

Since there was no jail in that little border town, Dorci was chained to the guards during the night. Again, though

Baju was dead, these men heard his stories as Dorci told them about his Hope. The next morning, a new detachment of four guards was assigned to escort him upriver to another village. As they trudged up the rocky barren valley, Baju spoke again as Dorci shared his Hope and the peace that is found in Jesus. That night he was chained to a new set of guards.

Although Dorci had become a captive of the Chinese Communist government, the Good News had not. In fact, the Tibetan guards themselves were now captives, for they, quite literally were chained to Christ in Dorci. For five days and five nights, with each change of the guard, God provided Dorci with a new congregation!

At the Administrative Center, Dorci languished in jail for two weeks while officials investigated the charges. As it turned out, they suspected him of being an agent of the Dalai Lama. When it became clear that he was just a Christian sharing the message of peace from the Prince of Peace, they turned him loose.

Back down the valley he went, and at each village, whenever God opened a door, Dorci stepped through, and again he used Baju's experiences to speak boldly of the faith. Still today, like Abel of ancient times, though his earthly body is dead, Baju's faith-filled life remains dynamically alive as it speaks to Tibetans who have never heard of this life-changing Hope.

I tell you the truth, unless a kernel of wheat falls to the ground and dies, it remains a single seed. But if it dies, it produces many seeds.
John 12:24

—An Illiterate Old Magar—
Lady

❧

CHAPTER 14

THE OLD MEDICINE LADY
ॐॐ

O osaha Boo-dhiya… the Old Medicine Lady. Now over eighty years old, that's what they call Darima. She acquired this nickname not from her age, but because she has learned the practice of walking with Jesus through many years of persecution and suffering.

In the fall of 1973, Baju gathered together four of his old soldier buddies, and shared with them the incredibly good news that he had recently discovered. Offering sacrifices they knew about. That was about giving blood to gods and spirits… to feed them… to satisfy them. They did it regularly.

If they were deadly serious, they would even carry out the five-blood sacrifice; a buffalo, a goat, a chicken, a pigeon and a duck. These animals, however, cost so much that it was normally done by a group of people… more often than not a whole village, and then only once every few years. But Baju was so religious, so serious in satisfying the gods, that more than once he gave the five-blood sacrifice at his own expense.

Now, however, he had learned that Jesus had offered Himself as a sacrifice, once and for all. And, it was not just to make some god happy, or to satisfy a dead ancestor with a meal of blood. It was to *take away* the sin of the whole world... including his... Baju's very own sin. When he shared this with his four friends, two of them immediately decided to follow Jesus. One of those was Darima's older brother, Khadak Bahadur.

Darima and Khadak Bahadur were from the same family clan as Baju. As children, they had grown up together in Arakhala. They were second cousins and in Magar culture they related virtually as brothers and sisters. Consequently, Darima and her husband, Prem, who lived on another mountain ridge, were strongly influenced by the changes in the life of that old soldier who visited them from time to time. The turnaround in the life of this derelict was so dramatic that it motivated them to embark on a search of the Bible for themselves.

By May 1979, we had been working with the Magar people for ten years, and Baju had been following Jesus for almost six years. No one else in Arakhala, however, showed any lasting interest. I had heard that Prem and Darima had learned of Jesus somewhere and were actively attempting to follow Him. In fact, they had chosen to be baptized the previous month. In those days of heavy opposition to the Good News, this was a very bold step. If the authorities so desired, the law was such that they could be imprisoned for three years.

Darima was totally illiterate. Prem, however, had been a British Gurkha soldier and could read and write. For the past three months, he had been having nightly meetings in which he would read the Bible. Many of his friends in the village of Chainpur were interested and came to listen.

Baju wanted to go see Prem and Darima again and help them better understand the message to which they had recently dedicated their lives. So one afternoon, he and I, along with a Christian young man from the plains, started down the mountain trail. I was very cautious and surely did not want to get caught in the middle of a village conflict over religion. Consequently, to keep as low a profile as possible, we timed our trip to arrive after sundown. As soon as it was light the next morning, we would leave… going off in another direction.

Upon arrival, I went straight inside Prem's tiny thatched hut where I would not be seen and sat down beside the smoky little fire. For the next few hours, Darima and her friends pummeled me with a barrage of questions about Jesus and the Bible. Before she was finished, I was so hoarse I could barely talk. Meanwhile, Baju had a small crowd of people around him, while our other friend had more with him in the loft of a little barn. We were amazed to find this many people so eager to hear the Good News in those days of persecution.

The Magar society is highly relationship orientated. Therefore, the primary focus is on maintaining harmony in the village. Being right or wrong is often not the primary question. In such a tightly integrated society where shamans and religious leaders hold great influence, and where expensive sacrifices are shared among the village, refusing to cooperate is a grave matter indeed.

So, Prem and Darima knew they were courting disaster. Their confidence in the love of God, however, had grown to the point that they could risk everything. They had placed the call of God above the demands of man. They reckoned that the only time they would truly not be safe was when they were not obedient to Him.

For the next three months, Prem's Bible readings continued until a nephew in the nearby village of Bhartipur went to the police. Then it all came to an end. When the police arrived, they took Prem, Indirya Kami and Dambar Singh Ale to the police station. During the beating, an inebriated policeman loaded his rifle and shoved it into Prem's stomach. Another policeman, however, pulled him away from Prem.

After twelve hours of continuous beating, they sent a message for Darima to come and retrieve her husband since he was unable to walk. She refused. The next day, the police dragged the three rebels back home. Prem's leg was bleeding pools of blood and the sergeant seemed worried that it would go bad for him if Prem died while in his custody.

A few days later the police were back. They needed to be paid for their work! They wanted compensation for all the "trouble" these three had caused them. In the end, each family came up with the four hundred rupees they demanded. A few days later they were back yet again. This time they insisted that Darima give them her large, very valuable goat. This was the last straw for her. She angrily told them they weren't getting her animal. Furthermore, they could cut her head off, but she would never leave Jesus. At this, they quit bothering her and Prem for a while.

A year or so later, Prem's mother died. When they buried her in a Christian manner, village persecution began again in earnest. They were given the village's worst punishment and declared *bahit*. This meant that, first and foremost, they were completely ostracized and humiliated by the village. They were declared to be lower than the lowest caste of untouchables. No one was allowed to give them water, and they were forbidden to use the village water source. They were not permitted to enter anyone's house, neither was anyone to enter their house. Furthermore, no one from the village was supposed to assist or help them in any way. In many respects, they were declared dead to the village. The duration of their punishment was set for six months, after which, it was assumed they once again would obey the village's religious rules.

Despite the punishment, Darima told me, there were points of encouragement during those six months. They had more rice fields than most, and harvesting was a huge job. Normally they would hire twenty-two people to do the work. Of course, everyone in Chainpur was strictly prohibited from helping them. However, some people from another village seized this opportunity to get employment. In all, fifteen men offered to cut their rice. They worked really hard and got it all done in one day. Consequently, their expenses were less than usual that year.

Afterwards, five people from their village risked being penalized. They offered to thrash their rice and carry it up the mountain to their hut. Part of the payment for this type of labor is feeding the laborers a huge meal at the end of the day. However, the Magars are strictly forbidden to eat food prepared by the low-caste, which the village had declared them to be. So again, the costs were all that much cheaper.

Darima was completely uneducated and just an untrained Christian believer. She was simple, yet intelligent and extremely hard-working, as many Magar people are. Regarding theology, she knew none whatsoever. What she did know, however, was to do the sorts of things that Jesus did. Consequently, she prayed, using the authority that she had learned was in Jesus' name. She totally understood that she herself had no power, so she let God… yes, she just relied upon God to use His power. She expected Him to do what He said He would do. And He did.

People with serious ailments went to the shaman or the other spiritual practitioners called the "blowers" for help. If these all failed, and they had some money, maybe they would go out to the plains to a medical facility. However, if they were not too ashamed to be seen around Christians, they might come to Darima. Her medicine was always free. She would pray for them, and Jesus seemed to have just the right diagnosis and the right remedy. And that is why she is known today as the Old Medicine Lady.

He called His twelve disciples to Him and gave them authority to drive out evil spirits and to cure every kind of disease and sickness.
Matthew 10:1

—Postscript—

Whether my presence that night provoked the beating of the three believers, I never learned. However, even more than thirty years later, I have yet to return to Chainpur Village. In fact, that was the only time I went out of my way to visit believers in another village. I was not concerned for my own health or safety. But, I could never be sure whether or not my presence might stir up a hornet's nest that these dear people would have to live with for years to come.

After a while, Prem's nephew in Bhartipur, the opposition leader who first reported them to the police had something happen to his knee so that he couldn't walk. Seven days later he died. This event cast a measure of fear over the villagers. It seemed to them that God might not have been happy with this man's hate for the Christians.

Before the year was out, the sergeant who was in charge of their beating also came to an unexpected end. He had gone out drinking one night, and while coming back along the trail he slipped and plummeted down the mountain to his death.

CHAPTER 15

THE CANCER

ॐॐ

All men will hate you because of me,
But he who stands firm to the end will be saved.
Matthew 10:22

Viciously, Rabi Lal kicked his wife. Over and over again, he kicked her. Then he beat her and dragged her away.

He just couldn't stand it. It was all so shameful… this Jesus thing. This foreign religion!

In the late 1960s, Darima's younger sister, Kanchi, and her family, had moved down to the plains. The government was making land available to settlers from the mountains, and the family had secured some fertile farmland across the road from their older brother Khadak.

In those days, there were very few Christians, and they were regularly accused of following a foreign religion. Consequently, Rabi Lal had forbidden his wife to attend meetings at the nearby church. And strictly speaking, she did not participate or only God knows what her husband might have done to her.

Instead, she would slip over to the tiny building and sit on the ground just below a little window. Then she would lean up against the stone and dirt wall. From there, she would strain to hear the words of singing and worship. And repeatedly, that is where Rabi Lal would find his wife before he dragged her away.

This was life for Darima's younger sister. Time and again she would sit under the open window, tears streaming down her face as she yearned to participate with the others... as her heart longed to worship Jesus. This was the closest that she dared to go. That is, until the cancer.

Rabi Lal was a retired Gurkha soldier and the army had provided him with some kind of help. However, now he had received all available treatment and in the end, there was nothing more to be done. The pain was everywhere in his body. He knew there was no hope, so there was only one solution. There was no point to wait any longer. He would jump into the surging Narayani River and end this awful suffering.

When Kanchi saw her husband take his bicycle out that day, she understood what was on Rabi Lal's mind. Racing out to the dirt road, she fought him for control of the bike. She was determined to do everything possible to stop him. When her brother, who lived across the road, saw what was happening, he too ran out to help her.

I didn't learn what particular conversation ensued, but the conclusion of it all was that Rabi Lal allowed Khadak to pray for him. By the time his prayer was finished, Rabi Lal was no longer hurting as badly as before, so he agreed to put his bicycle away.

Darima and her husband, Prem, lived over the mountains in their small hut on a ridge west of Arakhala. For some reason, the very next day Darima made that long trip down to the plains to visit her sister. When she reached Kanchi's house and heard what had happened the previous day, she had no doubt in her mind that her coming at this time was a Divine appointment.

Rabi Lal had exhausted every possible hope, and now he was willing to listen. He was willing to be prayed for, and this, Darima knew how to do. She began praying for him with a purpose. For her, praying could be short, or it could last for a long, long time. It didn't matter to her, and in such a crisis, this illiterate old woman was single-minded. In the course of the extended prayer, as it so happened with her from time to time, she said the Lord began to pray in, or through her. She didn't know what He was praying, but she knew it was just right. When her prayer was finished, Rabi Lal's body felt "light" and his pain had receded. In fact, he felt so good that he stood up, went outside and straightaway began repairing the roof of their little cattle shed. That was the end of his cancer.

—Postscript—

Darima, Kanchi and Khadak Bahadur Lungeli had grown up together in Arakhala Village. Soon after Baju became a follower of Jesus in July 1973, I became deathly sick and we returned to the U.S. Meanwhile, when Baju arrived home in August, he was eager to tell others about what he had experienced. He called together four of his old army buddies and told them the Good News. Khadak and one other old soldier became the first ones to respond to Baju's testimony. When Khadak died in 1983, the few Christians there on the plains staunchly refused to follow the Hindu death rites, and it precipitated another round of persecution.

Rabi Lal became a follower of Jesus and constructed a little building behind his house. Even to this day, it is still being used for church meetings.

Darima

CHAPTER 16

DEATH THREAT

*Everyone who wants to live a godly life
in Christ Jesus will be persecuted.*
2 Timothy 3:12

They were really fed up with Prem. He had absolutely refused to be reasonable… *refused* to cooperate.

The village council had already "shunned" him for six months. This meant that he and his family were treated as if they were lower than the lowest caste. No one was allowed to visit in his home, and Prem and his family were not allowed to step foot inside anyone else's house. No one was allowed to work in their fields or assist them in any way. The biggest trouble, however, was that they were not allowed to use the common water source.

In a society that has few resources and is chronically short of food, sharing is a regular and important part of life. If you have a little extra of something, you will share it. Friends and relatives were still allowed to do this. But when someone did bring them a gift, they were required to set it on the ground outside their house and leave it there. This was the village's way to heap more shame upon them.

The police had already beaten Prem and two of his friends mercilessly. His enemies had ridiculed and persecuted him in every sort of way, but still he would not listen. So this day, they threatened to eliminate him. In short, they promised to "feed" him a bullet. Perhaps now, he would come to his senses and once again do his part to contribute to the village sacrifices. Perhaps this threat would change his mind.

But it didn't. It just added one more trial to a long list of things that he and Darima would endure as they continued following Jesus. As it turned out, it wouldn't be Prem, however, who would "eat" their bullet. In the end, it would be his wife, Darima.

After the police had so brutally beaten Prem a couple of years earlier, he regularly went over the mountains to visit different hospitals. There, he searched for some relief from the aches and pains that so often afflicted his body. It was while Prem was away on one of those many trips that it happened.

Since the threat of assassination had obviously failed to intimidate Prem and Darima, one of their relatives went to the police again. He filed a report that they were refusing to join in the village sacrifices. They had abandoned their religion. Therefore, they were traitors to their country. They were followers of Jesus.

On the day the policemen arrived, however, both Prem and his closest friend Dambar Singh, happened to be out of the village. Not wanting to return to the police station empty-handed, the policemen decided to arrest their wives instead. After all, it was amply clear that

Darima and Tili Sara were equally guilty of the same crimes.

The following day, the police at the Dhobadi station escorted these two illiterate village ladies off to the District Headquarters where the governor himself could deal with them. At Headquarters, Darima and her friend were taken into a waiting room. When it was their turn, the secretary looked over the charge sheet. Then, he quizzed them about this foreign religion they were accused of following.

Darima, however, would not let his allegation go unchallenged. She made it very clear that contrary to common belief, this was not a foreign religion. It was not the religion of the white people. She knew quite well that some white people followed Jesus and some most certainly did not. Being white or foreign had nothing to do with it, she retorted.

The secretary wrote a note and sent it into the governor's office along with the charge sheet. In a few minutes, a note came back instructing him to send them home. When the secretary told them that they were free to go, Darima was dismayed. They had not had their trial. "We have come here, prepared to stay in prison," she protested.

She knew that their enemies would surely accuse them another time. Then, they would be forced to make that arduous trip all over again. Better to take the punishment now, she reasoned. "Isn't it possible to see the governor face to face?" she asked the secretary.

When the secretary agreed, Darima and Tili Sara carefully made their way into that large, imposing room. Darima was well over fifty and the governor, a college graduate, was much younger. With a smile and a twinkle in her eye, she told me how she didn't address him as "Sir," which is what custom would have required.

Instead, she kindly but fearlessly used the term *Babu*, meaning son. This is a term of endearment which indicated that she was relating to him as a part of her own family. If he did not protest, then he was accepting this arrangement. He didn't, and for all intents and purposes, this placed the governor in a relationship as if he were conversing with his own mother or aunt. After a few questions, he did indeed send them home.

The next morning as Darima and Tili Sara neared their village, they arrived at a huge banyan tree under which a number of people from Bhartipur Village were resting. It was they who had persecuted them the most, and the village where their relative lived who had filed the accusation.

These people were well-acquainted with the threat to "feed" Prem a bullet. Furthermore, they never expected to see Darima and Tili Sara out of jail for a long time, and were dumbfounded when the two ladies suddenly appeared. When they asked how they had been set free, Darima replied, "I 'ate' the bullet in my husband's place. I swallowed it straight down, and spat it out my bottom!"

This earthy description of how she had eliminated a deadly threat brought forth gales of laughter. As for their persecutors who were sitting there, it was a time of real chagrin. They had thought they had dealt the believers a serious blow. But instead, the governor himself had set the ignorant old ladies free. And to that, there was no recourse.

—Postscript—

Darima, Prem, Baju and the other Christians clearly understood their destiny and their place in the world. They were called to overcome the Kingdom of Darkness. That meant they had enlisted in an army that was engaged in nothing short of all-out war. War meant suffering, not a cozy, contented and peaceful life from which one slips painlessly into eternity. As a result, they were so secure, so confident in God's love that they gladly risked everything.

The record of the afflictions in the lives of Peter, Paul and other early Christians was clear. Consequently, the suffering and shame that was heaped upon them did not surprise them in the least. In fact, this met with their expectations of what a life of walking with Jesus would lead to.

The apostles left the Sanhedrin, rejoicing because they had been counted worthy of suffering disgrace for the Name.
Acts 5:41

—Two Stories from the 1980s—

ন৵৶

CHAPTER 17

THE HYENA

෫෫෨

It was a chance of a lifetime. Quite unexpectedly, an extraordinary opportunity had arrived for a young American boy. When men sat around the fires telling their stories, he would be remembered as a hero in Magar folklore for decades to come.

It was April 1986, and as usual, it was hot in Arakhala. The villagers had pressed me that day to go hunting with them, but there were other things on my mind. Baju was working with me to revise 2 Corinthians, and I did not want to miss any time with him on this very difficult epistle. As always, meat was very scarce in the village, and the men told me they had high hopes of getting some meat to eat that day. Reluctantly I agreed, and Michael and I set out along with ten other men.

All day we scoured the rugged western face of Peak-of-the-gods, but failed to come across a single mountain goat or barking deer. About two o'clock in the afternoon, I excused myself and left for home. I was in very good shape and could jog down off that steep mountain in thirty minutes. In another hour or less I could make the 1,500 foot climb up the ridge to Arakhala.

Meanwhile, the men continued to hunt. When they started for home, they descended to the streambed. At that point, for some reason Michael traded out the little .22 rifle he was carrying for Jeepan's 12 gauge shotgun. Jipan went off to adjust the water flow to his small rice terraces that were nearby and everyone else went over to the stream to refresh themselves.

A few minutes later, they were all sitting in the shade on some large boulders when loud screams and shrieks jerked them to attention. The commotion was coming from behind a knoll on the opposite side of the little stream. A large hyena had been after a lady's goats, but she had seen him before he had killed any. With all her yelling, the hyena had backed away and trotted around the hill.

Now he appeared on the edge of a terrace, only fifty yards away from Michael. After Jeepan and me, Michael, aged twelve, was perhaps as good a shot as anyone else in the village. Resting the gun on one of the many rocks, Michael would have no difficulty making a killing shot on a target of that size.

The hyena was standing right in front of him, but Michael did nothing. He just sat there, unmoving. Meanwhile, three other hunters ran towards the hyena.

Blaaaaang!

Blaaaaang!

Blaaaaang!

The great blasts from their old hand-crafted muzzle-loaders echoed back and forth throughout the canyon. Huge billows of smoke filled the air from their home-made black powder. When the acrid clouds drifted away, it was as we had come to expect... not a hair on the animal was touched!

Unlike a jackal, the hyena is much larger. They are very bold, and this one seemed to pay no attention to the hunters. After a moment, he took a few bounds up the mountainside and sat there looking back before he finally disappeared into the thick brush.

Actually, the hyena probably didn't sit down... it just appeared that way. Compared to a jackal, the hyena's face is more in the shape of a dog. Its large front shoulders and smaller hindquarters with upright head often give it the appearance of sitting down.

In years past, leopards, wolves, tigers, as well as bears, hyenas, and terrifying pythons have made their homes in the forests around Arakhala. But by the 1980s, continuous deforestation had led to the demise or relocation of most of those animals. Occasionally we heard of the odd tiger from nearby Chituwan National Park passing through the area. And although I had heard about hyenas before, this was the only incident where I was absolutely certain that it wasn't a wild dog or some other animal.

Later, we were to learn that just a day earlier a hyena had attacked Baju's goats in this same area. This one, however, moved on and presumably filled his stomach with goats from other villages for we never heard of him again.

From olden times, stories of hunting exploits would be repeated around the fire at night. Had Michael dispatched this fearful predator, he would have become one of the heroes among the Magar hunters... not only in

Arakhala, but in a multitude of villages up and down the Kali Gandaki River Valley.

But it was not to be. He was unprepared. He had the bullets for the .22 rifle in his pocket, but his gun was with Jeepan. He had Jeepan's shotgun in his hand, but the shotgun shells were with Jeepan. It really wasn't his fault. Nevertheless, both weapons were useless! Michael had learned an important lesson… be prepared.

—Postscript—

In his book, *Tigers of the Raj*, Colonel Richard Burton makes mention of the many times he encountered hyenas in India. On page 38, he tells of a man-eating hyena which he killed in 1907, to the great joy and relief of the local villagers.

Once the hunters had come off the mountain, no one expected that there would be anything to shoot. "Be Prepared" is the Boy Scout motto which Michael had memorized. But just saying something with your mouth is far different from doing it.

It is one thing to be prepared to deal with a savage predator. It is far more important, however, to prepare for eternity and for when we will meet the King. Otherwise, we might find ourselves sitting on the sidelines while the chance of a lifetime passes us by.

The Bible insistently teaches us about being prepared. The way to be prepared, of course, is to always be listening to God… always searching for more of Jesus. If we walk with Him, as He urges us to do, we will be prepared to deal with every trial and evil thing that comes our way. Then we will learn how to respond to each crisis, and our spiritual ears will be in tune to hear Him say,

This is the way; walk in it.
Isaiah 30:21

Striped Hyena

CHAPTER 18

THE IMMIGRATION OFFICER
❦

"**Y**ou have to go back to Penang and get a visa!" the Thai immigration officer declared sternly. This had never happened to us before and it was a real shock. I thought to myself, "I can't cope with any more stress right now. This is just too much!"

Barbara and I had been staying near the Dalat School where Michael was studying in Penang, Malaysia. We had been unable to secure a resident visa for our project in Nepal, so we had left there a couple of months earlier. Since then we had been moving from place to place and living out of our suitcases.

Now we were planning to go to Bangkok and apply for a thirty-day Tourist Visa at the Nepal Embassy. As usual, money was short, so instead of flying we were riding the overnight train from Penang to Bangkok, and had just reached the Malaysia-Thai border crossing.

In the past, we had always been given a visa upon arrival in Thailand. However, this time the officer had told me that I would not receive a visa at his border post.

This meant we would have to abandon our seats on the train and return to Penang. Once we had gotten a Thai visa there, we would have to buy train tickets all over again. But now, it was just a few days before the Chinese New Year celebrations were to begin. The huge crowds traveling over the next two or three weeks would make it impossible to get a seat. Who knows when the next reservations for that long, overnight train ride might become available? In addition, I would miss out on crucial consultant help at a conference in Thailand.

When we had reached the Thai border, all the passengers tumbled out of the train and handed in their passports. Then we stood in a large crowd outside a little office while two immigration officers processed all six carloads of passengers. After some while, an officer began to call out names in a strongly accented voice. Everyone strained to hear above the babble and try to make out whether his name had been called. When I guessed it was my name, I pressed through the crowd and reached out my hand.

It was then that I heard those shocking words, *"You have to go back!"*

I took my passport from him and just stood there. As bad as the situation appeared, incredibly, I wasn't overwhelmed by thoughts of what to do. Tired... yes. Dejected... yes. Shocked and surprised... yes. But no fear, no anger. God's eternal promise was still at work. *There is no fear in love. But perfect love drives out fear* (1 John 4:18).

It wasn't that I saw anything, but nevertheless it was as if an angel of the Lord was there beside me. The peace in my heart did not leave me, even though we were worn out and heavily stressed by our constant moving. Even though I was completely mystified by this sudden turn of events, I carefully reminded myself, "Gary, with God, there is always a way! The Coach has a plan."

By all accounts, I should have gotten myself going and pulled our bags off the train right then and there. After all, somehow, somewhere I would have to find a bus that would take us back to Penang. Instead, I just stood there... contemplating, waiting, unwilling to accept my fate... at least not immediately. After a while, Barbara's passport came forth. We were surprised, however, when the officer didn't tell her also to go back.

I continued to stand there in the midst of this crowd that was jabbering away in languages completely unknown to me. I wondered what God would have me do. I needed to hear from Him. I needed His promised wisdom. After a while, the Thai officer spoke again. "I told you before! You have to go back to Penang!"

This time, however, it seemed obvious that he wasn't speaking to me. It was someone else in the pressing crowd that he was looking at. As I processed this new piece of information, it dawned on me to look into Barbara's passport. Though we couldn't read the Thai writing, we could see that she had a blurry Thai stamp in it and presumed it to be a visa. We were still in such a state of shock that it was hard for me to think clearly. Finally, we thought to look in my passport. For some reason, there was a stamp identical to hers.

Why was that, we wondered?

We had no idea.

We talked it over and over and finally presumed that despite the official's statement, somehow a visa had been stamped in my passport by mistake. So we climbed aboard the train, wondering if at any moment an officer might appear to escort me off.

A few minutes after the train pulled away from the border station, another traveler, a young white pregnant lady came up to us. She was curious how I had managed to get back aboard the train. She had been standing right beside me in the crowd, she said. She had heard the immigration officer tell me to go back to Penang.

I told her that it seemed like there was a Thai visa stamped in my passport, but I wasn't altogether sure. I brought out my passport and asked her to show me hers. Sure enough, her blurry stamp appeared to be the same as mine. Wow, was she surprised... and so was I. The only thing I could figure was that the Thai official was multi-tasking and that he had a habit of looking at one person while conversing with another.

But the bigger surprise was that despite the fatigue and shock, His peace never left me. Certainly that peace wasn't of my own making.

Peace I leave with you; my peace I give you.
John 14:27

—Postscript—

We were so thankful that we hadn't taken the Thai official's word at face value. Otherwise, we would have left the train and gone back to Penang. I had relied on and followed God's peace in my heart, rather than the obvious words of the official. Satan was certainly hard at work in attempting to discourage us, but we had crossed this hurdle and passed the test.

—My Time of Great Loss—

(1991-1992)

CHAPTER 19

THE PROCESSION

❧

(As witnessed and written by our friend
Harrold Andresen, Dallas, Texas)

December 7, 1991

Silently, and in orderly fashion, the cars filed out of the church parking lot. I stopped at the street, thinking that the police officer would let the five or six cars that were waiting pass. Not a chance. He motioned us on as if he wouldn't even consider such a thing.

Two or three blocks went by as we traveled the six-lane boulevard. No other traffic could be seen. What a perfect time for a funeral procession. Then we crested a hill and saw the intersection in front of us. Cars were backed up in each direction ten or fifteen deep. Maybe this wasn't such a quiet day for a funeral after all.

We turned south on Cockrell Hill Road. This main thoroughfare on Saturday afternoon should have been heavily traveled, yet the entire roadway on the opposite side was vacant. I rolled down my window in amazement. Where could all the cars have gone? And how could it be so still and quiet? Then I noticed that the far lane was packed bumper to bumper. Somehow, all the drivers decided to pull completely off the road and park at the side, single file, leaving two lanes completely empty for as far ahead as I could see.

As we passed, I noticed many with windows rolled down, and some standing beside their cars, heads bowed. The unnatural silence was suddenly shattered for the second time as a motorcycle escort raced ahead to block another intersection. I'd never seen a procession like this... block after block of silent motionless traffic, interrupted only by the low-pitched drone of the Harley police bikes as they blasted by. I thought, "There's more honor and respect shown here than at the funeral of President J. F. Kennedy. This is incredible!"

My eyes filled up and my throat started to tighten. The Lord seemed to whisper, "Barbara *is* a famous and important person in *My* kingdom!"

For the next two or three blocks, I just tried to control my tears enough to drive safely. At one point, I could almost see the front of the procession, four blocks ahead, and headlights behind us for at least six blocks with the cars still coming around the corner. This was no little event. My wife asked if I was all right, but I was too choked up to answer. We were approaching an extremely busy, main intersection and I thought we'd be stopping soon, so I could regain my composure.

The intersection was in view now. Cars were backed up for two or three blocks, yet we were given the exclusive use of the road. There wouldn't be any stopping for us. Even the oncoming lanes were completely still. This time it was bumper to bumper, in all three lanes. The freeway exit ramp was jammed up all the way back to the overpass. Yet silence prevailed. No horns beeping, no signs of impatience, no butting in line. Many people were standing beside their vehicles. "But God," I thought, "these people don't even know Barbara!" And the Lord immediately answered, "But all My legions of angels in heaven know her, and they would certainly want these few people on earth to show at least this kind of respect."

The procession continued, still in perfect single file, unbroken formation, never stopping. First we passed the busy Target parking lot, then the K-Mart store. Again cars were stopped everywhere. Cars were even stopped in traffic lanes that wouldn't interfere with the procession at all. Yet somehow, by God's incredible power, He seemed to have issued the decree, "Hush! Be still!"

I resigned myself to blurred eyes and a knotted throat, still amazed at the hundreds of reverent people we had just passed. I thought, "You couldn't pay enough to get that many people to show such sincere and genuine respect on a busy Saturday afternoon." He replied, "My love is more effective than any amount of money."

My foot went for the brake as a rich lady in the white 1991 Cadillac began to pull out into my lane. I was sure this perfect procession would have to stop. But before I could even slow down, she had already forced the shift lever into Park and was rolling down her tinted, power window. As we passed she pulled off her jewel-studded glasses, and I think I saw a tear in her eye. "Certainly she's got places to go and people to see," I thought, "and she probably isn't used to stopping for anyone." She could have easily backed up and gone another way... but there she sat, in reverence.

At Wheatland Road we turned right. As far ahead as I could see, the left hand side of this divided, six-lane road was strewn with cars. The sight was most unusual. Unlike the first part of Cockrell Hill Road, where everyone pulled completely off to the right lane and stopped in single file, here it looked like someone had just turned off the power all at the same time. Cars were stopped halfway through a turn. Some were right in the middle of a lane. Others were sticking partway out of a side street. It looked like everyone had instantly frozen in the wake of the silent and solemn procession. "Why do you think these cars are all stopped in the middle of the street?" Nancy asked, as she was suddenly struck with the uniqueness of what she was seeing. I was almost able to answer, "Only God could have orchestrated anything like this."

We passed the Fire Hall, the Police Station and the Public Library... they all seemed so small and powerless. Then, in silent and continuous form, we turned left down Santa Fe. Parked in the middle of the opposite lane was a beat-up old paint truck, with ladders tied on the roof. The painter was standing beside the truck with one hand on the opened door, and the other holding his splattered paint cap over his heart... a common working man, on a busy Saturday afternoon, showing sincere and genuine respect.

As we wound through the final stretch of wooded residential area, I thought maybe my face would dry and throat unclog before we arrived. But then there was the silver Porsche, halfway out of the driveway and into the street. The metallic paint on the streamlined nose of the car glistened in the sun. It brought memories of the twelve years I had spent working on those types of cars before moving to Dallas to serve the Body of Christ. That's the kind of car that can make anyone who drives it feel instantly important, powerful, big-headed and in charge of the road. It's a high-powered German sports machine that won't let anything get in its way, especially with that teenaged-looking driver behind the wheel. His side of the street was completely empty as the procession approached from the opposite lane. Yet there it sat, exhaust pipes silent, the driver's eyes looking sullen. Only the God of the universe could stop that kind of combination for Barbara's friends to pass by in peace. I felt like a guest of honor. Tears were warming my cheeks again.

Up ahead, I could see the cars making the final turn into the cemetery. A lady was walking her dog along the grassy shoulder. She stopped, pulled her dog close, and bent down on one knee as we passed. "Lord," I exclaimed, "This is absolutely too much!"

"Oh, He replied, "This is nothing!! Wait until you see a real homecoming in heaven!"

CHAPTER 20

IDENTICAL SCARS

ॐॐ

That day in a crowded barroom, an assassin waited. He had a problem, however, and that was to aim his small pistol accurately while at the same time keeping it concealed. Pretending to occupy himself with his drink, the hired gun waited patiently for an opening between him and his victim.

Bang!

A man staggered, and fell to the floor.

In the weeks and months after Barbara's sudden death, many, many times I felt so lonely. Nevertheless, God was my steadfast companion. Often He used me to comfort, encourage, or direct someone's attention to the Kingdom of Heaven. This day, however, would be more unusual than any other.

I had just traveled halfway around the world, coming straight from Nepal to my hometown of Oak Harbor, Washington. When I arrived on Monday evening, March 2, 1992, a message from Pastor Steve Schell awaited me.

The following morning, I phoned Steve and he asked if I would come down to south Seattle the next day to speak at their Wednesday evening meeting. As usual, I felt beat-up and half depressed from the long, long journey and eleven hours of jet lag. I tried to work out another date, but he needed me tomorrow.

The next morning I rented a car. From Oak Harbor there are two routes to Seattle. Usually I drive south down Whidbey Island and take the ferry over to the mainland. I particularly like being on the ocean water, and the ferry ride gives me a little rest during the trip. For some reason though, I decided to take the longer way and drive north over Deception Pass. This road would take me across three bridges and two more islands before I reached the mainland. There, I would get on Interstate Highway 5 and head south to my destination.

At Burlington, the on-ramp makes an S curve that climbs up onto the freeway. As a result, I was not going very fast when I saw him. A young man with a backpack stood there by the signboard, obviously looking for a ride.

Over the previous twenty-five years, I had never picked up a hitchhiker. But today, with no forethought, I pulled off the road and stopped. The hitchhiker threw his backpack on the rear seat and jumped in beside me. Once on the highway, I assumed that we would pass the time away chatting, but when I tried to make light conversation, he barely responded. It quickly became apparent that he was really down and out. For the first half hour, there were long periods of silence between my questions, so I used these interludes to pray before I asked him something more.

Eventually I learned that he was from Montana, was twenty-four years old, and loved to fish and hunt. That was good for me. The first memories of my life are about fishing. He showed me a picture of his little son and beautiful wife. Little by little I learned that he was a construction worker. Some time before Christmas, he had finished a project and had arrived home a day early to find his wife with his best friend. At nearly the same time that I lost Barbara, he, too, lost the love of his life.

The hitchhiker, however, hadn't accepted the obvious. Among other things, he had a one-year-old son he dearly loved. In the following months, he desperately tried to make his wife happy. However, just two weeks earlier he had discovered her in a barroom with yet another man. Feeling that all hope was gone, he had given her a divorce and everything he owned: his pickup truck, his work tools... everything. Then he stuffed a few clothes in his backpack and walked out onto the highway to look for a ride.

He hitchhiked across Montana, Idaho, and Washington State to nearby Orcas Island where he stayed with his grandmother. Now he was going down to Portland, Oregon to stay with a friend who could help him find a job.

Aching for his little son and lonely beyond words, the hitchhiker was trapped in a quagmire of hurting, hopelessness, and confusion. Since we had well over an hour of driving before I would turn off the freeway, I began to tell him some of my hunting and fishing stories.

I was just about his age when I had committed my life to following Jesus and my most astonishing experiences had happened in the years after that. One time there was the fishing trip in Canada with Erv Bergmann. In less than twenty-four hours, we had caught twelve huge King Salmon. The smallest fish had weighed in at 25 pounds, and the largest weighed 55 pounds.

One of Gary's King Salmon

Then there was the time I had returned from Nepal so weakened by disease that I couldn't hold up a cup of coffee. Nevertheless, a month later, after a pleasant, thirty-minute stroll in a beautiful spruce forest, I had shot a bull moose at 25 yards.

These stories cheered him up, and I got him to tell me some of his hunting and fishing experiences. At last I came to the best story of all... the amazing grace I had experienced when I had been shot down four years earlier. (See "Dead on Arrival" *Angel Tracks in the Himalayas,* Chapter 31). Now the hitchhiker really came out of his shell. It was no small matter to be shot through the middle with a 165 grain expanding bullet and survive. Being a hunter himself, he had no trouble recognizing that I was a living miracle. I finished up the story relating how I laid in the hospital, hovering between heaven and earth for 48 hours, while God was so close that it seemed I could all but touch Him.

About that time, the young man turned toward me and began tugging at his shirt. When he had pulled it up, he showed me his own scars... a bullet hole in his side and a long incision where the surgeons had split him open from his rib cage to the bottom of his abdomen.

His scars were identical to mine!

A couple of years earlier, he had presumably saved the life of some unknown person when he stepped into an assassin's line of fire in a crowded barroom. The .22 bullet was only one-fifth the size of the bullet that had blown me down. And though he was right in the city of Las Vegas and not far from a hospital, still he had barely survived. The bullet had gone through his middle, ricocheted off his pelvis and into his other organs. He had lost his spleen, ten feet of intestine, and part of his kidney. Yes, he too had been shot down and had lived to tell about it!

As we approached the exit that would take me to Northwest Church, the hitchhiker asked me to drop him off some place where he could get some water. It was then that I asked him about food and money. He had neither. His grandmother had made him something, but he had eaten it earlier. He would reach his friend's house in less than a day and a half, he said, and he would be okay without food until then. Up ahead I saw a restaurant, and pulled in so he could get his drink of water.

As he was leaving the car, I promised that I would pray for him… if he would tell me his name. He brightened up once again and replied, "Scott. It's Scott Burton."

I slipped him a $20 bill in my handshake and told him that the Lord wanted him to have something to eat. When he thanked me, I replied that this was the Lord's money. He was the One to thank. I asked him then if he could get a Bible, and find out for himself what God had to say to him. He promised he would do that.

—Postscript—

For God, the odds mean absolutely nothing. As I thought about it later, it is incredible to suppose that this meeting happened merely by chance. God had brought a devastated young man across three states to stay with his grandmother. Then He had kept him there for ten days, while I traveled halfway around the world.

Next, He had prompted Steve Schell to ask me to come down to speak on just that day. After that, He put it in my mind to drive the longer way around to Seattle… in order to meet the hitchhiker… a young man in desperate need, who had gotten on a particular ferry from Orcas Island… a man who was to find a ride with someone who would drop him off at the Interstate 5 freeway on-ramp less than five minutes before I arrived. There, for the first time in 25 years, I would pull my car off the road to pick up a hitchhiker… one who had scars identical to my own.

I have never seen Scott since. When we parted he said that he hoped to see me again, but he never asked for my name and I didn't offer it. In any event, I expected to spend most of my life in Nepal, so meeting him again on earth was even more unlikely. Nevertheless, he didn't have to know me. If he got to know my friend Jesus, He would lead him out of his hopelessness and into a productive life that gave him joy and meaning.

My supposition is that He did.

Over the years, we have learned that in spite of our own pain, some of the strangest things happen when we ask God to make us a blessing to others. This was just another occasion where God was clearly my companion. Even when one feels desperately alone, like I often did in those days, I was reassured by the fact that I never was, and never will be really alone!

The LORD your God is with you,
He is mighty to save.
He will take great delight in you,
He will quiet you with His love,
He will rejoice over you with singing.
Zephaniah 3:17

CHAPTER 21

MICHAEL'S GIFT

ॐॐ

I had traveled thousands of miles in order to be at Michael's high school track meet that day. He had told me he would be competing in the 400-meter relay race, as well as the high jump at the Georgetown All-City Track Meet. However, as we sat in the stands watching some of the events, he announced, "Dad, I'm not running today. Nathan is running in my place."

From previous contests on Penang Island in Malaysia, Michael knew the competition. "Don't worry, Dad," he said, "I'll do okay. I'll get a medal in the high jump."

As for the relay race, he explained that there were two boys at their little boarding school who were lightning fast, and they fully expected their team to break the city record. Another boy, as well as Michael and Nathan, was also fast. Five boys had been selected for the relay team... one was to be the backup, in case one of the four became sick or was injured. Nathan was that fifth man. Even though he was training morning, noon, and night, he still had not been able to outrun Michael.

Michael had been on the volleyball and soccer teams, and he excelled in wind surfing, diving and other events at school. But in sports, Nathan's best was being fifth man on the relay team. This would be his only chance in high school to win a sports medal. So, Michael had chosen to forfeit this opportunity to have his name written in the record book. Instead, he would sit with me in the stands and cheer them on.

"I wish Mom was here to watch me jump," Michael said to me.

We were still hurting deeply from her tragic death four months earlier. I reminded him of the reference in Hebrews 12:1 about the great crowd in the heavenly grandstands. It wasn't like having her here, of course, but wanting to encourage him I replied, "I think she's probably watching."

During the relay race, the Dalat School boys had difficulties passing the baton and they came in third. However, the first and second place teams stepped outside their lanes and the referees disqualified them. The Dalat boys were awarded first place after all, and Nathan earned a gold medal!

But to our surprise, Michael did, too. He hadn't realized it, but in Malaysia the fifth man stood on the winners' stand with the team and received a medal along with the four who had run.

As for the high jump, Michael did his best ever. Georgetown was a city of 800,000 people, and that day he took first place. He had earned one gold medal in the high jump, and had received another gold medal for sitting in the stands cheering for Nathan.

Michael's Gift

Later, at the State Track Meet, Michael jumped even higher, also taking first place there. Even though he had experienced profound sorrow from the loss of his mother, he had not forgotten how to give.

And God hadn't either.

Jesus said,

> *Give, and it will be given to you.*
> *A good measure, pressed down,*
> *shaken together and running over...*
> Luke 6:38

Baju gives Michael a khurpa knife for Christmas

CHAPTER 22

THE MISSING PART

*There is a time for everything...
a time to weep and a time to laugh,
a time to mourn and a time to dance.*
Ecclesiastes 3:1, 4

Why does life feel so difficult when a person we love dies? Why does one feel so sorrowful, so lost and so sad?

When I lost Barbara, I often wondered why the pain was so deep. Now almost 20 years later, I think I have some insight into why I felt as I did for so long. Actually, as I think back, I realize that even after things were beginning to go rather well and my spirits were really up again, there was still a very deep sense of loss and sadness in my soul. The pain, however, didn't seem to have to do with the shock that her death was unexpected. Rather, it was the fact that now I was alone and I felt a vast emptiness in my heart.

135

Part of the reason for our sadness, I believe, stems from how God has made each of us individually. We can readily recognize how our children reflect the temperament, and often the likes and dislikes of one or both parents. In a similar manner, we humans in our great diversity reflect something unique and special about our Heavenly Father. This is even more apparent with those whose lives reveal the indwelling Holy Spirit. In a mysterious way, our loved-one has been, in some way or another, God-in-the-flesh to us. They weren't God, of course. But certainly they were children of God.

As such, it could be said that God loved us, God touched us, and sometimes even spoke to us through that person. Therefore, when that person goes to heaven and leaves us behind, something of God dies to us. Intuitively, deep down we realize that this unique God-ness will never again touch us and love us in that way until we meet again in heaven. There, God Himself will fulfill all that that person was to us, and immeasurably much more.

Consequently, I believe that a significant part of the pain of loss, as well as the resulting mourning, has to do with the fact that God made Adam and Eve in His own image. God's plan, as illustrated in the Garden of Eden, was fellowship with Him. There, He could walk and talk with Adam and Eve. Every day He came and walked alongside them, sharing with them and enjoying together the good things of life. This was meant to last forever... until Satan deceitfully came and stole God's family away from Him.

So at least part, maybe a large part, of why our hearts feel that loss so very deeply is that we have lost something very tangible of God. It is right, therefore, and proper for us to be deeply grieved. That, in my opinion, is an honor both to the person, as well as to their Father God.

With each person being so different, it is impossible to say how long it will take before that grief significantly fades away. I was blessed that God sent me Kerry to fill a large part of what I was missing. Soon after I went through my ten days of tears, I was able to begin looking forwards, rather than backwards (See *Angel Tracks in the Himalayas* Chapter 43).

I decided that whenever we had an opportunity, I would talk with Michael and Adina about "Mommy." We would remember her foibles and failures and laugh. We would share and relive her goodness and love... and particularly in the early months of our grieving, with tears. We still talk about her when occasions arise. The result is that our hearts and minds have become all the more fixed on the future, and heaven has become more appealing to each of us.

Blessed are those who mourn,
for they will be comforted.
Matthew 5:4

CHAPTER 23

WHY?

ॐॐ

As you do not know the path of the wind,
or how the body is formed in a mother's womb,
so you cannot understand the work of God,
the Maker of all things.
Ecclesiastes 11:5

After all the wonderful answers to prayer we had experienced, why did Barbara not recover? Why did she have to die so tragically? Why wasn't she healed?

Baju also used to ask similar questions. Many times I heard him say, "Why do our people keep sacrificing to their useless idols? Why hasn't Arakhala turned to the Lord?" Then with a chuckle, Baju would always answer his own question saying, "Ah, it's just not the right time, I suppose."

Even though his only son showed no response whatsoever to the Good News, Baju never seemed to lose hope or get exasperated at God's apparent tardiness in answering his prayers. Baju's overwhelming gratitude for the forgiveness of his sins fostered an unshakeable trust in God, and this kept him from the trap of dwelling on the "why" questions.

Baju no doubt, had learned from Job's experience in ancient times that it was not helpful to demand that God explain Himself. In Chapter 3, five times Job asks the question why? "Why was I born? Why didn't I die in infancy?"

Later, Job continues with more "why" questions. But when God joins the conversation in chapter 38, He ignores Job's whys. Instead, for over one hundred verses God queries Job with questions about the world that Job cannot answer. The meaning is clear... if you cannot answer these simple questions, how can you expect to understand the whys?

Baju's favorite Bible verse was, *Ask and you will receive* (John 16:24). What we ask for, however, can make a huge difference. Asking God "why" is often unproductive, and likely to be ignored. Think about it. How much information would we have to know to fully understand why? The fact is that just like God, we would have to know everything.

In conversations with his friends, Job eventually arrives at the answer himself. *Where then does wisdom come from? Where does understanding dwell? ...God understands the way to it and He alone knows where it dwells* (Job 28:20, 23).

In any event, God does not require us to know all things. Neither does His plan necessarily include satisfying our intellectual curiosity. Rather, His plan is that we have enough information to trust Him. When we learn to trust Him, we will learn to love Him. When we learn to love and enjoy Him, we readily become an active participant in the Kingdom Business.

In the final book of the Bible, the Book of Revelation, the question "why" is never found. Rather, at the end of time we see the great multitude of saints standing before the throne of God along with innumerable angels and the twenty-four elders (Revelation 7:9-12). From this holy congregation a great chorus is heard saying, *Praise and glory, wisdom and thanks and honor.*

In heaven we will see the whole picture. Then the answers to "why" will be self-evident. God's strategy will be so incredible and so amazing that rather than asking why, our response will be an awe-filled, "Wisdom and praise and glory to our God!"

The wisest man of all ages addresses the why question at least four times. (See Ecclesiastes 3:11; 8:17; 11:5; Proverbs 20:24). King Solomon's summary is... *you cannot fathom the work of God.*

The Psalm writer, Asaph, also sought to know why. He reported, *When I tried to understand all this, it was oppressive to me* (Psalm 73:16). His wise conclusion to the matter declared, *and being with You, I desire nothing on earth* (Psalm 73:25).

In heaven, "why" will never be heard. Meanwhile, for our fleeting time here on earth, we will do well to seek for, and be contented with, His Presence.

It is to the glory of God to conceal a matter.
Proverbs 25:2

With regards to heaven, Jesus said,

In that day you will no longer ask me anything.
John 16:23

—Postscript—

Thanks to Pastor Gary Hutchinson, Arlington, Texas, for sharing the why/wisdom connection at the funeral of Janice Miles.

—New Beginnings with that Nurse—

(1992-2003)

CHAPTER 24

CAPTURED IN KATHMANDU
ॐ

'I know the plans I have for you,'
declares the LORD,
'plans to prosper you and not to harm you,
plans to give you hope and a future.'
Jeremiah 29:11

I was about to be captured, and I didn't have a clue. Though I struggled hard to escape, it was a done deal and God was in it. He knew it was coming, and it was all His plan... a plan to bless me, not to curse me.

Ten days earlier, life had been blissfully uncomplicated. I had been in Kathmandu collecting information on how to build a mountain road over the steep Mahabharat Range. During this time, I was attentive to unplanned meetings, of which there were many. Most of them had to do with sharing God's comfort and loving-kindness to me following Barbara's death.

That summer, however, had been disastrous. Thirty days apart, two large jets had crashed into the mountains surrounding Kathmandu. Everyone was killed, including a missionary family on each plane. Consequently, God had brought a number of brokenhearted people across my path. In sharing about my own grief and experiences, they, too, had received comfort from God.

With these tragedies in mind, my friends, Paul and Norma Seefeldt, had invited me to their home one Sunday night to share with their grieving friends, Kirk and Paula Dunham. Meanwhile, Norma was taking seriously my need for a partner in my work in Nepal, and she was praying and listening for the Lord's direction. In fact, she had someone in mind for me to meet. Unfortunately, however, that lady was out of the country. That was okay with me, and anyway, I was focused on sharing the comfort of God that night. After dinner, as Norma and Paula were taking care of the dishes, they simultaneously had a revelation. Immediately, Norma came out and emphatically declared, "You need to meet Kerry Brown. She's the perfect match for you!"

"Well, whatever," I thought.

I had never heard of this Kerry Brown. I was told that she was a nurse and midwife who had worked for a number of years in some remote villages around Nepal. At the time, I had no interest in any of the single ladies in the country. If I met someone new, I was sure that she would have friends. "Who knows," I thought, "where that could eventually lead?"

As a result, it was arranged for me to join the Dunhams for dinner at their home on Tuesday, November 3rd to meet that nurse. When Kirk gave us a ride back home that evening, to my surprise, I discovered that this nurse was living only ten houses away, on the very same narrow lane as me.

For a couple of days some bug had been upsetting my stomach. So with that as an excuse, the next morning I dropped into her clinic. I thought I was pretty much in control of myself, but apparently I was much more nervous than I thought. When she checked my blood pressure, it was sky high! Nevertheless, somehow I managed to invite her out for dinner on the coming Tuesday. After all, I suggested, maybe she could give me some pointers about what medicines to take out to the village (as if, after 23 years I didn't know).

That weekend I had some necessary work to finish up in Arakhala Village, so I raced out across the mountains and back as fast as I could. At dinner together on Tuesday night, she told me her whole life story... the good and the bad. I was supremely impressed by her perseverance and faithfulness to God's call, as well as her honesty regarding some serious problems and difficult situations she had encountered. She wasn't perfect, but unquestionably she was an overcomer.

Two days later, on Thursday, we were to go out to dinner again. I certainly enjoyed her company, but when I reassessed the situation, I realized that this relationship was moving ahead far more quickly than I had anticipated. I had promised my children, Adina and Michael, that I would be with them for Thanksgiving and Christmas. So, the very next Friday I was booked to fly back to the U.S. In December, Kerry was returning to Australia for home leave, and she would not be back for nine months.

It did not take an Einstein to figure out that the next eight days were not long enough for us to get to know each other. It seemed so obvious that I should not have stirred up false hopes and invited her out to dinner a second time. Now, however, I just had to make the best of it. I had gotten myself into this pickle, and I was ready to bail out. Perhaps something might come of it ten months later, I thought.

Somehow though, I had botched it completely… I had forgotten about God. I had failed to remember my prayers when I had pleaded with God to deliver me from the "dating game." Over the previous eleven months, this silent prayer had been uttered a thousand times or more. However, if God were to answer my desperate prayer, and if I refused to do the dating thing, how would I find a partner? I had never considered what the other options might be.

Now though, I was only focusing on my present problem. I needed to get a confirmation from God regarding my decision to cut short this budding relationship. As I was reading my Bible that morning, my eyes stuck on 1 John 3:21-22,

Dear friends, if our hearts do not condemn us,
we have confidence before God
and receive from Him anything we ask,
because we obey His commands
and do what pleases Him.

As I analyzed the phrases, I first considered my heart. What was happening there? All was well. There was no condemnation and nothing was out of line. To the best of my knowledge I was following Jesus and doing what pleased Him.

And what was it that I was asking of God? Obviously, it was for a companion for the rest of my life. The missing piece here was confidence. That was a different matter. I was bewildered and I had no confidence about what was happening. It seemed to me as if suddenly I was driving my car much too fast. Somehow, I felt like I was going to end up in a fiery crash!

I should not have been fearful, however. Many times I had experienced God's admonition that *my thoughts are not your thoughts, neither are your ways my ways,* (Isaiah 55:8). But it seems I had forgotten this, and I was greatly alarmed. Throughout the day I continued to ponder the verse that I had read early that morning. To my consternation, the more I thought about it, the more I found confidence growing in my heart.

In those days, I walked to most places around Kathmandu. It was a good way to get exercise, as well as to help reduce my blood pressure, which had gone too high after Barbara's death. By the middle of the afternoon, I pictured my feet hitting the sidewalk as solidly as a rhinoceros tromping the jungle trails of Nepal, and this confidence began to make me very concerned indeed.

Well, I knew what to do about that. I would have God fix it. He knew that this whole thing was absurd. Obviously, one cannot have a life-changing decision of this magnitude come together in just a few short days. So I began reminding God that He had to take this confidence away. If He did not, it was going to be His fault! And, by the way, I told Him, He only had until 6:00 p.m. to do it!

That evening, still with two minds, I knocked on Kerry's door. In my heart, confidence had taken over and was beginning to reign. But in my analytical mind, I was still full of doubt. Was I being irresponsible with the rest of my life? I was not sure. But then, where did this confidence come from? I knew that I was unable to work up such assurance with the strained abilities of my own heart. How could it be so powerful? It had to come from God. Or did it?

Over dinner Kerry quizzed me about my past, and I spent the night telling my life's story... including the years when Barbara had suffered periods of depression, mental illness, and her eventual suicide. Back at Kerry's apartment that night we were drinking coffee, when at a pause in our conversation, she asked me what I was thinking. This was fast becoming serious and my hands began to shake. Taking her hand I prayed that God would give clarity to our conversation. Then I proceeded to tell her how greatly I had been impressed by her faithfulness to God, and by her perseverance to overcome. Of course, I never mentioned how completely I had chickened out earlier in the day.

At this point, we were deeply into speaking the truth. When I was finished, I asked her what she was thinking. I noticed now that it was she who was trembling, so I took her hand and prayed again. She told me that she was not desperate to get married, but I would do!

(Well, for a joke that's what I tell friends nowadays. Actually, she did not say that at all. However, being forty-five years old, having turned down three proposals and never married... anyway, back to the real story.)

She knew about me and Barbara from my book *Life Among the Magars*, printed in 1982. But she had never seen me until eighteen days earlier when new arrivals at church were asked to introduce themselves. The following week, more than once my name had appeared, scrolled before her eyes, and she was wondering what my future might be... and whether I could ever be interested in her. Then, eight days later, she had received a phone call from Paula to ask if she would like to come to dinner and meet an eligible man. From the moment we met at the Dunhams' home, she was thinking about me so much that she had been unable to sleep.

This amazed me. I really needed help now, so I suggested that we pray again. We kneeled down together and I asked God to make clear His direction for our lives, and to show us if His plan included a future for us together.

Friday night we were over at Norma and Paul Seefeldt's house for dinner. On Saturday, we strolled out to the empty fields beyond the city and leaned against a stack of dried corn stalks. The sky was sparkling blue, and to the north, God stretched out before us the snow-covered Himalayas in an extraordinarily stunning panorama. That afternoon we shared our goals and dreams of what the future might hold in each of our lives.

At this point, I no longer felt plagued as I had earlier in the week by the nervousness of being around her. However, I had completely forgotten about my constant prayer of the preceding months, when I had asked God to rescue me from the "dating game." Dating might be okay for those who were twenty or thirty. But I was fifty-one, and I could not stomach the idea of getting to know one lady really well, then another, and then another. So, I had asked God to save me from that emotional roller coaster. It had never entered my mind what God might have to do to answer my prayer. It would take a meditative person such as Norma to pray month after month, and then emphatically declare, "Kerry Brown is the perfect match for you."

Secondly, it would take a promise I had made to myself. I had determined that I would never kiss another lady before I had asked her to marry me. This promise was about to be broken. Back at her apartment that night we were continuing our all-day discussions, and sitting rather close, when she kissed me!

Now, I was out-of-bounds! What was I to do? I was desperate to correct it... and fast! Unable to come up with another idea, I asked her to marry me. With no hesitation, she said, "Yes!"

Later on, that nurse claimed that it was not she who had kissed me. However, I certainly know that I had no plan whatsoever of kissing her. I did not feel that I was in love with her. I was simply struggling to discover God's direction in my life, and then she kissed me. She, however, claims that she was only responding to me. The truth is that we do not know any more. So, we have agreed that it was all just a part of God's plan.

Neither of us foresaw this happening so fast... and here I was leaving Nepal in six days. We really did not know each other, but we had agreed to get married. God, however, had given us peace and I never had any concern about it, nor did I ever have second thoughts. She had a heart of gold that she had offered first to God, and now to me. God had brought this attractive lady into my life, and we trusted God that our love would grow with time... and it did.

So, this is the story of how my heart was captured in Kathmandu in 1992. Four months later, on March 13,

1993, we were married in Melbourne, Australia. At the time, it is fair to say that we were fully committed to one another, but we really fell in love in the following weeks as we got to know each other better.

We were surprisingly different in quite significant ways. The things I liked best were usually outdoors. Hers were indoors. There were also many differences we did not anticipate between the Australian and American cultures. Even though there wasn't sufficient time to hurdle them all before our wedding, we were not disturbed about them. We were absolutely convinced that God had a plan to bless us. He had a plan to give us a future and a hope. We had promised to spend the rest of our lives together, striving to become one heart and one mind. We now looked forward to that with great anticipation, and with real joy.

—Postscript—

Kerry would not replace Barbara, nor could she ever. But, as I often reminded her, she could and she would inherit all that was Barbara's. Many people admonished us not to live in Barbara's house when we returned to Dallas. Consequently, I readily offered to sell it, but Kerry was not sure that this was God's plan. She wanted to try living there first to see what God would do. She held strongly to God's promise that *I can do all things through Christ who strengthens me* (Philippians 4:13), and we live there still today.

Interestingly, when we are in conversation with friends from thirty or forty years ago, I may misspeak Barbara's name when I mean Kerry. That, however, does not bother her at all. She has never felt a need to compete with Barbara. Through Barbara she has inherited two children, Adina and Michael... and now six grandchildren. They all love and appreciate her greatly. Barbara laid a good foundation for the family, and Kerry has continued to build upon it. We, and the grandchildren, feel very much indebted to her for this. We are all so grateful to God for "that nurse" who captured me with a kiss that night in Kathmandu... and I continue to love and appreciate her more deeply as the days go by.

November 14, 1992
(This turned out to be our engagement picture.)

CHAPTER 25

THE MAGARS' ROAD

પ્ર~~

The request seemed really far-fetched. It was far beyond our capacity and the idea seemed certain to fail. Nevertheless, we felt we should at least ask the Lord for direction, and in the end, Barbara and I felt that God would have us try.

For over twenty years we had been doing our best to help people in this remote area, but most of our efforts enjoyed only marginal success. The grinding poverty and the constant oppression of the high caste Hindus had produced a pervading attitude of helplessness among the Magar people. They aimed at short-term survival, and generally ignored our new ideas for change.

Year after year we had helped great numbers of sick people with modern medicine. Otherwise, only two other projects seemed to have made any lasting difference: the drinking water systems bringing in clean water had significantly reduced disease and the new varieties of seed we brought in had produced much larger harvests of corn, rice, and millet.

From our beginning with Wycliffe, its founder, Cameron Townsend, had challenged us to reach out into the backwaters of society in practical ways. In the early years, he would send me an encouraging note from time to time, or even a few hundred dollars to do something helpful for the Magar people.

Now in January 1991, General Baral had asked us to build a road over the precipitous Mahabharat Range. General Baral had earned his Masters Degree in Economics, and he insisted that all economic progress was built upon the foundation of transportation and communication. Whether it was raising silk worms, growing a large variety of garden vegetables, or keeping rabbits, most of my many projects had eventually come to naught for one reason or another. This, he suggested, was largely due to Arakhala being in a remote area with no transportation.

To build a road is one thing. But a mountain road across the foothills of the Himalayas? This was something that seemed incredibly difficult. For over two decades we had been trekking these mountain trails and were intimately acquainted with their steep, rocky slopes.

Even if we discovered a feasible route, which seemed doubtful, where would I find the finances to build it? No government aid agency would ever put that much money into my hands. Wycliffe could not help, and I didn't know anybody who had ever attempted such a thing before. At General Baral's insistence, however, we agreed to try. His plan was to establish a non-profit organization, to be named Deuchuli Hills Development Association. Local leaders would form the committee to guide the work, and I would be the advisor. (Deuchuli at 6,200 feet is the highest mountain in the area. Translated, it means Peak-of-the-gods.)

Over the next four months we made some initial investigations. But in May 1991, Barbara had a severe mental breakdown and we returned to the U.S. I thought she was recovering well, but in December she took her life. At that point, I had no plans for further work in Nepal. Eventually, however, the caring encouragement of others helped me realize I still had work to do with the Magar people.

In November 1992 I was back in Kathmandu to move forward with plans for the road. It was then that I was introduced to Kerry, and that halted our road project again. After our marriage in Australia in March 1993, we returned to Dallas and traveled around to visit friends and supporters in the U.S. A crucial break came when a long-time friend, Loren Berry, gave me a small hand-held level that he was using to build logging roads in the steep mountains of Northern California.

Back in Nepal, I taught my best friend, Jeepan, how to use it and sent him out to find a way over the Mahabharat Range... if, in fact, one existed. Looking up at those sheer mountainsides, it was patently obvious that there would be no simple route. Everyone assumed that unless we had millions and millions of dollars, this was just a fairytale dream. Over the next two years, Jeepan would work out a route and then we would change or modify it. After four major changes, we discovered a way that might possibly work.

A $4,000 gift from Samaritan's Purse at that time gave us sufficient money to do some trials. The situation was such, however, that the government would certainly not allow us to acquire dynamite. The major question was whether the Magars could build this road with just their primitive hand tools. I need not have doubted, however. The Magars broke up the rock with sledgehammers and chisels, and they leveled the roadway with hoes and shovels far more efficiently than I could have ever dreamed.

Knowing that the Magars could do it now, we set out to find the finances. In the spring of 1994, we traveled to Washington, D.C. where we met Bud Hancock, founder of Enterprise Development International. Not unlike Cameron Townsend, Bud was a visionary and he fully understood our hopes and dreams. The obviously high probability of failure didn't trouble him at all.

Bud realized that as long as the Magar people remained poverty stricken, everyone would continue to suffer. We dreamt that if somehow we succeeded in pushing a road through, it would promote a significant economic development in the area. Among other things, the few beleaguered believers might be freed from the grip of abject poverty. Perhaps then, they could develop their own resources to reach out to other Magar villages.

Historically, the Magars were regularly cheated out of what little money they had... usually with the temptation of alcohol. To circumvent that, we paid the village workers with rice. This way their hard labor would fully benefit their destitute, hungry families.

Enterprise Development International adopted and supported this project for the first three critical years of road construction. Then some of our own friends provided resources to complete the road that became known as Barbara's Highway. The road opened in late 1998 By

2010, magnificent changes had occurred, far and beyond all we had hoped or imagined.

When jeeps and tractors began to carry goods over the pass, tons and tons of rice were immediately carted into this food deficient area. The cost of transporting cargo dropped from seven rupees to one rupee per kilo (2.2 pounds). Along with a variety of other items, sheets of galvanized roofing were also brought in. As a result, one by one the thatched roofs in the area were replaced with metal roofs. This protected them from the dreaded fires that could totally destroy a whole village in an hour or less.

The thick grass roofs also housed hordes of rats, so as the grass roofs disappeared, the rat population dwindled. Others have told me that rats would have destroyed twenty to forty percent of the corn, rice, and millet in those homes. So, the net effect has been to save three months' worth of their available food supply every year.

In addition, the five to six weeks of exhausting work needed each year to cut thatch and repair and replace roofs has come to an end. Now they can make better use of this time. Among other things, they have been building cement toilets, and are also getting their crops planted at the optimum time. Since the villagers are no longer required to carry enormous loads over the mountains, their overall calorie/food requirement has been appreciably reduced... not to mention the considerable wear and tear on their bodies.

Each of these changes by itself would not make so great a difference. But together, there been a multiplying and accelerating effect. After my open-heart surgery in 2000 we were gone for two years. On our return, we clearly saw a major improvement in the overall health of the people. Sickness was greatly reduced, and the people were no longer skinny and haggard.

Also, there are no less than three unplanned consequences of the road. First, the road made it possible for heavy materials to be transported over the pass, and a number of small hydro-electric plants have been installed, bringing light to many, many villages in the region. Secondly, because there is enough food to eat, families don't require their children to work in the fields to the same extent, so the schools are now overflowing with students.

Thirdly, there is a natural reforestation of thousands of acres. Over the decades, I felt a deep sadness when I saw beautiful virgin forests, great rhododendron trees, and giant tree ferns burned to ash. I tried everything I knew to protect them, but it was useless. The people were desperately hungry and they had no alternative. Once they had enough to eat, however, they began to abandon their slash and burn agriculture. Today, when I look out at these mountains, I see great sections of dark green where reforestation is taking place naturally.

In the end, we spent about $250,000. The eighteen-mile road that opened up this valley reached eleven villages. Local government and village initiatives have added to Barbara's Highway in the succeeding years. Like a spider web, little roads now run in every direction. In fact, one can even reach the main highway near Narayanghat in the east, as well as Tansen in the west. I haven't been able to accurately measure it, but I could guess that an additional 200 miles of arterial roads lace through the mountains, reaching another eighty or more villages. And this is being added to almost monthly.

In the early days, General Baral, who loved Barbara like his own daughter, insisted that the road should be named after Barbara, who gave so much of herself for the Magar people. Today, there is a sign posted at each end with the words, "BARBARA ROAD." I call it Barbara's Highway. Villagers constantly remark about how it has lifted the load of drudgery and the crushing burden of poverty from off their shoulders. As a result, the debilitating attitude of hopelessness, which used to pervade village society, has nearly vanished.

And a highway will be there;
It will be called the Way of Holiness.
Isaiah 35:8

—Postscript—

Three people were critical to the success of the project. The first was General K. J. Baral. His ancestral village is just up the mountain from Arakhala. He looked after government relations and made it possible for the work to even begin. He had culminated a distinguished career in the nationwide police force by serving in the top position as Inspector General for six years. Afterwards, he served another six years as Nepal's ambassador to Burma. And later still, he was the United Nations' Special Envoy in charge of the Peace Force in Cambodia for two years.

The second person was Captain Lal Bahadur Thapa, a retired Gurkha soldier from Arakhala. He purchased rice and tools, and meticulously looked after the money and bookkeeping. The third was my special friend, Jeepan, who marvelously and tirelessly performed the mammoth job of surveying, and later, supervising the workers. I had known each of these men for some twenty years, and I knew that their integrity was beyond reproach. This unique team, their individual abilities, and their total dedication to serving the village people, made the project a success.

*Jeepan and General Baral in
Arakhala Village*

Captain L.B. Thapa

Jeepan

164

Cutting out 85 feet of vertical rock by hand

Sledgehammer and iron chisel

Part of the finished road

June 13, 1998

Our jeep on the first trip to Arakhala.
It was the first vehicle ever to reach this
remote part of Nepal. Some villagers had
never seen a motorized vehicle before.

CHAPTER 26

THE OLD BEGGAR LADY

❦

May 1995

Misty rain was falling that dull, grey morning when she came. It was just after dawn and I was planning to sit down with a cup of coffee and quietly read my Bible. But first, I would pick a few flowers for Kerry, I decided.

The front yard was separated from the street by a high, cement block wall. Most Nepalis could not see over it, but when I was up close, I was just tall enough to look onto the road. No one was about... just a very short, wizened old Poon lady clothed in traditional tribal dress. Shuffling along slowly, she was neatly but simply attired, her grey hair in tight braids coiled on top of her head.

I picked the last flowers and was headed back inside, when I passed by our front gate. It was then that she saw me and called out. Reluctantly, I turned back. Her deeply wrinkled, bronze face appeared creased with pain and sure enough, she had a story and wanted some money!

She claimed she had gone to the doctor two days earlier for an intestinal problem. She had used every bit of her money... eighty rupees, on the doctor and on medicine. But now she was worse off than before, and she was on her way to see him again. She was a widow and her only resources were two daughters... and, of course, they lived in far-off Kathmandu.

We had just moved to that quiet, narrow street in the town of Pokhara only a couple of weeks earlier, and were not yet familiar with the local alcoholics and derelicts. So, I decided to foist her off to our neighbors, the Swarbricks. They would recognize her if she were a regular deadbeat or drinker. But when it became apparent they were not up yet, I checked my pocket.

Bummer! I only had one fifty-rupee, and one one-hundred-rupee note. I calculated that the doctor would cost her fifty rupees or less. Stuffing the hundred-rupee note back into my pocket, I reluctantly stuck the fifty rupees through the grated iron gate. Cupping her weathered hands and bowing her old grey head in respect and thanks, she gently took my money.

In those days, beggars were at our door practically every day, and normally I gave them something. The deadbeats were the real problem. On receiving any gift, they became obnoxious and always asked for more. If I refused to give extra, the conversation could turn decidedly unpleasant. It was most irritating. I hadn't read my Bible yet and I wanted a good start to this day!

Dropping the fifty into her hands, I spun around quickly and headed for our back door. If she said anything, I had determined I would just pretend I didn't hear and keep on going. As I was moving quickly away, I heard her softly murmur, "Thank you Jesus! Bless this person and his house!"

At that time, there were very, very few Poon Christians in Nepal, and I knew of none living nearby. My baffled brain began grappling with what I had just heard. I was already a good way to the door when the thought came to me, "Jerk!" I chastised myself, "You should have given her a hundred rupees so she could have gotten some medicine as well!"

I stopped, dumbfounded, mulling it over in my mind. Then I turned and ambled back to the gate, intending to give her my hundred-rupee note as well. I looked down the street to call out to her, but she wasn't there. I could see clearly into the yard next door, as well as into the yard across the street. There was no one in sight. She had vanished.

I had muffed this opportunity to bless a poor, needy soul, and I felt decidedly sad. Meanwhile, I was mystified at how this sickly old woman, who had been shuffling along so very slowly, could have disappeared that quickly. I will meet her again on the street, I reassured myself. Or at least, as others had done before, as soon as she is well she will come back to thank me.

In the days and months ahead, I yearned to meet her and kept a careful lookout, but I never saw her again. As I pondered it all, little by little the tiny details of the encounter began to form a unique picture. It took on a pattern with a fragrance that is referred to in Scripture:

Some have entertained angels unawares.
Hebrews 13:2

—Postscript—

The old widow lady had prayed much like Baju... short, so direct, and powerful. It seemed that she had a direct line to heaven. At the time, we were facing strong opposition from certain political leaders who were trying to prevent us from building a road into the Magar villages. So we surely needed a friend like her praying for us, I thought.

The ensuing fifteen years were times of civil unrest, revolution and increasing lawlessness in Nepal. In times such as these, our house was often empty for months at a time. Though there have been no less than six attempts to break into the house, not once were they successful. In retrospect, the beggar lady's prayer of blessing on our house seems to have been extraordinarily effective!

CHAPTER 27

A NEW FREEDOM

❧

Punishing the children for the sin of the fathers to
the third and fourth generation of those who hate me.
Exodus 20:5

My language helper and friend, Baju, had often shown me by example how to forgive and bless your enemies. However, I had not fully grasped the gravity of this principle until now. Finally though, I had faced the truth, and it brought me face to face with a heart-wrenching dilemma… my sin would have serious consequences for my children and grandchildren!

To be honest, this was a sin I had persistently ignored. For the past thirty years, whenever the Holy Spirit would bring it to mind, I had always made excuses and shrugged it off. Year after year I had refused to heed the Bible warning. Instead, when I couldn't avoid the subject, I managed to convince myself with some clever mental gymnastics that this warning wouldn't apply, of course, to a "good" and committed Christian such as me.

However, I could no longer avoid the obvious. At this moment of truth, it was up to me to decide the inheritance I would impart to my children and grandchildren. Decades from now, what fruit would my life produce? Would it bring them blessings, or would it bring curses?

It wasn't that I didn't want to obey God. Rather, quite frankly, it was simply that I relished this sin more than obedience. If, however, Jesus were to be my example, how could I continue to make these feeble excuses? How could I selectively obey His word only when it suited me?

In retrospect, the underlying problem was that I couldn't understand God's plan. I now realized, however, this was no excuse. After all, if I were able to understand everything He planned from beginning to end, then I would be like God. I would be equal to God.

It had all begun one day with that niggling part in the Lord's Prayer which said, *Forgive us our sins, for we also forgive everyone who sins against us* (Luke 11:4).

When I tried to avoid its application, I read Jesus' straightforward explanation, *But if you do not forgive men their sins, your Father will not forgive your sins* (Matthew 6:15).

Then there was the application of this principle in the story that Jesus told of the servant who owed his master millions. The master, incredible as it seems, found the compassion to completely forgive the enormous debt. Soon thereafter, however, the forgiven one came across a fellow-servant who owed him a small debt and had him thrown in jail. When the master learned what his ungrateful servant had done, he revoked his forgiveness, and had him imprisoned and turned over to the tormentors.

And again, just in case I wanted to weasel out of this teaching… and I did… Jesus finished His story by plainly explaining the application. *This is how my Heavenly Father will treat each of you unless you forgive your brother from your heart* (Matthew 18:35).

Peter, the apostle, thought that forgiving someone seven times ought to be sufficient to fulfill the forgiveness requirement. But Jesus wouldn't let him off. Instead, He told Peter to forgive seventy times seven times! The point was that forgiveness had to be like our Heavenly Father's… without reserve… without end.

Theology is one thing. But in real life practice, this just didn't seem fair… at least not in some cases. Isn't God supposed to be just and fair? Where was justice? In those days, there was a case where someone had been exempted from the law and completely excused. This goaded me ceaselessly.

That wasn't right. It wasn't fair. And month after month, every time I thought of him my blood pressure skyrocketed.

Now, however, I was face to face with the facts. Jesus plainly stated that those who loved Him would obey Him (John 14:23). Clearly, unforgiveness is disobedience, and disobedience is sin. Furthermore, according to Exodus 20:5, sin is something that will affect my children and my family for generations to come.

Lastly, I knew better than most that Satan prowled around like a roaring lion looking for defenseless victims to devour (1 Peter 5:8). I certainly needed every shield and fortress that God had made available to me. Without a doubt, I desperately needed to remain under the protective wings of God's love. Obviously, one did that by being obedient (John 15:10). Jesus' life, of course, was a prime example. For three years His enemies were constantly trying to kill Him, but He kept doing exactly what the Father commanded Him (John 14:31). And time after time, He escaped from their clutches.

That day, I realized that the alternatives were not good. Satan would surely find increasing opportunities to defeat me at my weak points. This in turn, would directly affect the spiritual, as well as the physical wellbeing of me and my family.

It was clear to me now. My example of selective forgiveness could not be hidden. My children and grandchildren would see it. Almost certainly they would do as I had done; obeying Jesus in the areas that were convenient, while making excuses for the rest. Consequently, the peace of God which passes understanding and guards our hearts and minds, would just be an elusive promise that regularly slipped from their grasp.

But God knew this person deserved to be punished! Wasn't it right to expect justice, and hope that some evil would befall him soon? That, it became clear, was not God's perspective. Jesus died for all sins. The eternal plan, the Father's hope, was that he too would find repentance and forgiveness one day... not judgment.

As I began to study it, I realized that I was doing the same sort of thing that Satan had done in ages past. Just like him, I had tried to climb up on God's throne (Isaiah 14:13-14). By my actions, not only had I tried to take His place, I had also spoken forth judgments as if I myself were the Almighty Judge.

That attitude, that pride, would rub off on my family. That is, unless I put a stop to it. The choice was mine. It was not easy, but it had to be done unless I loved my sin more than I loved my children. Sin… my sin, would have consequences far beyond myself.

Likewise, repentance and obedience would also have their consequences. Those consequences would be in the present as well as in eternity. Obedience in everything would prove to God, as well as to others, the genuineness of my love for Him. In times of deep trouble and great crisis, God promised that my love would be remembered.

In retrospect, I realized that Satan had deceived me and I had been blinded to the truth. I had mistakenly felt that by forgiving, I somehow gave approval to someone's misdeeds. But "feeling" that way didn't make it true. I didn't have to approve of this person's actions to forgive him. When my little children were messing around and spilled their milk, I didn't have to approve of it to forgive them. The milk was still lost, and we still had to clean it up. But that was an entirely separate issue from the one of forgiveness.

Furthermore, withholding my forgiveness didn't affect this person in the least. On the other hand, my continuously simmering anger certainly did affect me and those around me!

It was hard. It was real hard to obey Jesus like this! Forgiveness had to be genuine, and it had to become a habit. In the coming days, I sometimes found it required an emotionless, hard, cold decision of my will. But nevertheless, I did forgive that person from my heart. Eventually, forgiving became an established habit. Jesus had set me free! Sin no longer held me captive.

It is for freedom that Christ has set us free.
Galatians 5:1

—Postscript—

I had to learn to relate to others according to their need, just as God does, rather than according to the pain they have caused me. In releasing all judgment to God, I was moving aside and affirming that He could, and would see to it that one day justice would prevail. I was giving up my right, if I had one, to extract payment from the offending party.

The next step, however, was one in which Baju excelled. That was to pray for God's blessings upon one's enemies. Until the day his chief nemesis the witchdoctor died, Baju prayed for him. To overcome evil with good is what would truly make me more like Christ. Blessing my enemies can do real damage to Satan's realm. That is what God's Kingdom is all about. That is what I had to be about… all the time.

Bless those who curse you,
pray for those who mistreat you.
Luke 6:28

CHAPTER 28

THE DEMONIZED GIRL

∂∞∞

'Lord, have mercy on my son,' he said.
'He is an epileptic and is suffering greatly.
He often falls into the fire or into the water.'
Matthew 17:15

February 15, 1997

S atan, it seemed, held all the cards.
Sareeta's condition was critical. And just as we were about to pray, the drunken headman from the nearby village barged in. Obviously, the devil had the upper hand, and we were trapped in a quandary. With this fellow creating such a ruckus, how could we hear God? How could we pray effectively?

Now, sixteen days later, we were returning to that little tea shop with thoughts of dread hammering my mind. As Kerry and I toiled up the dusty trail that crossed the rough Mahabharat Range, I couldn't help but wonder, "Will Sareeta still be alive?"

I was sure I knew the answer. If she were not dead, without God's intervention, there was a high probability that she would be severely injured. Epileptic fits were well-known by the villagers, but I knew of no one in these mountains who had survived them for long. Inevitably the victim would slip off the trail and tumble down the mountain. Or, he would roll into the fire, or fall from a tree. If the person didn't die immediately, his injuries would be a foretaste of a lingering and ghastly death.

Two weeks earlier, we had trekked out from Arakhala and crossed the pass. Halfway down the mountain to the plains, we stopped to rest at the tiny thatched hut tea shop owned by Manee Ram and his deaf wife. Living with them were two delightful granddaughters, the oldest being twelve-year-old Sareeta.

We were well acquainted with the girls, and when Sareeta entered that little, eight-by-twelve foot space, she looked appalling. Her eyes were itchy, red and full of pus. This condition was not unusual in the mountains and we often carried some medicine with us. We were always careful, however, not to presume that the villagers wanted our medicine or our help.

I asked Manee Ram if he would like us to treat her. Yes, she would like that, he said, but what she really wanted was medicine for her epilepsy! That was a huge shock to us for we had no idea that she was an epileptic. This, we learned, was a new development. In fact, for the past six weeks she had suffered dreadful seizures six or seven times a day. In addition, because of the turmoil this created, she had been expelled from school.

We were in an impossible position now. Yes, we could find medicine for her... somewhere. But this could be a lifetime condition, and there was no way to have it properly administered. Looking at this charming little girl, we felt so deeply sad for her, so totally helpless.

After discussing our options at length, we told him that we would not be able to get her any medicine. It just wasn't feasible. The only help we could offer was to pray.

"Yes!" he replied. "That is just what she wants!"

It turned out, he said, that in the nearby village a lady with a very serious condition had recently been healed when Christians prayed for her. So, this too, was Sareeta's fervent hope.

Peatam was carrying our stuff in a basket on his back that day. Since Baju's promotion to heaven the previous year, there was no one in Arakhala who walked closer with God than Peatam. Leaving Kerry and Peatam to do what they could with Sareeta, I went over to distract the headman. Together with Sareeta's grandfather, we did our best to maintain some semblance of order in that tiny room.

It was a real predicament. We desperately needed to hear from God. We needed discernment. We needed to know God's plan. We needed to pray in high faith. Considering Sareeta's pitiful situation, it all seemed to be a very unsatisfactory time of prayer. Her chances of surviving for long were simply nonexistent. With all the commotion, Kerry and Peatam had only been able to offer a short, simple prayer, and had to leave it at that. What else could we do?

Now we were returning, dreading what we might find at that little tea shop perched beside the mountain trail. After a long, hard hour of climbing we crossed a now bone-dry brook. Soon thereafter, we topped the eastern shoulder of a ridge and followed the trail that circled through a tall, mahogany forest up to Manee Ram's place.

Then, through the trees we could see her... standing in the sun beside the grass hut. She had been watching out for us, and when she saw us coming she began waving. What a relief! What joy it was to see her alive and well!

When we reached the tea shop we were thrilled to learn that she had not experienced another seizure since we had prayed. Unfortunately, we couldn't linger there for long. The steepest, most difficult climb on that hot southern face of the mountain was still ahead, and after a cup of tea we departed.

It would be many hours before we would reach Arakhala Village. Despite the withering heat, the great joy in our hearts lifted our feet almost effortlessly on that grueling climb to the pass. As we crested the range, we commented to one another that it felt as if we had just floated up the mountain that day on wings of joy and thanksgiving. Great is our God and greatly to be praised!

> *Jesus of Nazareth was a man accredited by*
> *God to you by miracles, wonders and signs,*
> *which God did among you through Him.*
> Acts 2:22

—Postscript—

In wanting to pray the "right way," we had failed to keep in mind that God looks at the heart, rather than at the formula of our prayer. Furthermore, we had failed to fully grasp the meaning of asking in Jesus' name. When we asked the Father to heal Sareeta in Jesus' name, it was simply that... for the extension of Jesus' kingdom. Jesus had come to destroy the devil's work (1 John 3:8). Healing her that day, perfectly met those criteria.

Kerry and Sareeta

After that, every time we saw Sareeta, Kerry reminded her that she couldn't worship other gods any more. It was Jesus, and none other, who had healed her. She and her grandfather were both thoroughly convinced of this. However, some time later we stopped in only to learn that Sareeta had had a seizure that very morning! This discouraged us, and Kerry went to find her. She discovered that there had been a celebration of a Hindu god that morning, and Sareeta had been forced to join in the worship. Shortly afterwards, she had another seizure!

A couple of years later she went to live with her father and his new wife. One day, he too forced her to partake in the worship of a Hindu god... and it happened yet again. From then onwards, she insisted on living with her grandfather. In the following years, she strongly resisted any such pressure, and has been free from epilepsy to this present time.

And I will do whatever you ask in my name,
so that the Son may bring glory to the Father.
John 14:13

CHAPTER 29

TWO TRANSFORMED LIVES
෧ඐ

I n over twenty-five years the tiny old lady had never spoken a word to us. Their small tea shop/home was at the base of the mountains, and often we would stop in there on our trips to Arakhala. She was all but completely deaf, so her husband had to shout at her to fix us tea. Once that was done, she would stand back with a somewhat puzzled look on her face, while he did all the talking.

Over the years, Barbara gave medicine to the family for various problems, and prayed for them from time to time. Whatever it was, Barbara's kindnesses impacted them both very deeply. After Barbara died, old Manee Ram begged us for a picture of her. For them, she was a saint. In his Hindu Brahman way, her picture was displayed high on their wall where he could revere it and pray to her spirit. Later, when Kerry and I would come up the trail, Manee Ram would plead with us to stop for a while, and often we did. Without fail, he would point to

Barbara's picture and tell us some remembrance of her, expounding upon the greatness of her soul.

Forty years earlier, Manee Ram and his wife had settled on the edge of the plains where he was allotted a substantial plot of fertile land by the government. Though he was hard-working and very intelligent, the whiskey bottle had gotten the best of him. Over the years, he sold off all his land to buy alcohol, and we only knew him as pitifully poor and often inebriated.

When we started building the Magar road, Manee Ram could see that more travelers would use that route, so he built a tiny grass hut part way up the mountain. There, the people coming and going could buy tea and cookies as well as something more substantial to eat... and always, there was the alcohol. Helping them, were two delightful granddaughters who had been abandoned by their mother.

Ten years earlier, Peatam and Kerry had prayed for the eldest granddaughter, Sareeta, and she was delivered from terrible attacks of epilepsy. Unlike many villagers I have known, Manee Ram clearly understood that it was only by the power of Jesus' name that his granddaughter was not only alive, but also completely well. It took some years, however, before he was able to grasp the fact that it was possible for a completely hopeless person like himself to be forgiven by God and find healing for his soul.

When his life began to change, I must admit that I was rather reluctant to rejoice in his verbal professions. I was wary that one day my hopes might be shattered by his return to the bottle. His faith, however, was most genuine,

Kerry with Manee Ram and his wife

and in the last couple of years the radiance of his largely toothless smile has only continued to increase.

After a two year absence, we saw him briefly on our way up to Arakhala, and upon seeing us he clapped for joy. Then on our way out from Arakhala, we decided to take time out from our long journey back to Pokhara to have a cup of tea with him. When we stopped there, he was nowhere to be found. I supposed that his old wife had more or less learned lip-reading, so speaking to her in Nepali and using the common hand signs, I asked where Manee Ram had gone. To my astonishment, instead of replying with hand signs, she answered in the sweetest tone, "Oh, he has gone off to Kirtipur."

I called for Kerry, and she came over and began to talk with her. They had such a joyful chat and the new sparkle in her eyes gave us no doubt that she too had grasped the immense significance that Jesus' blood cleanses us from all unrighteousness and gives us a peace that passes understanding. It was some twenty-five years in coming... but now she was hearing both us and God.

Then will the eyes of the blind be opened
and the ears of the deaf unstopped...
Gladness and joy will overtake them,
and sorrow and sighing will flee away.
Isaiah 35:5, 10

—Postscript—

February 15th, 2009

Since that last trip, we have returned to Arakhala again. On our way back to Pokhara we stopped at the bottom of the mountain to have tea with Manee Ram and his tiny old wife. The transformation, the excitement and joy that radiated from these two nearly toothless, wrinkled faces thrilled our hearts. They have been transformed by the freedom they have found in Jesus. Manee Ram never stopped talking about how wonderful life has become now that he knows Jesus. His dear wife was beaming as well, and I was able to have a conversation with her. Though she still has some hearing impairment, it is nothing like it was before.

February 22nd, 2009

Sunday morning, 7:30 a.m., a week after we saw him, Manee Ram phoned us in Pokhara to say goodbye. We were returning to America, and since he is old he feels that he may not see us again. He certainly knows, however, the assurance that we will meet again in heaven. He expressed over and over how much he loves us.

Later, Kerry and I discussed the significance of this call. Kerry was moved to tears as we thought about God's goodness and grace in allowing us to see the continuing transformation in the lives of this impoverished, but precious old couple.

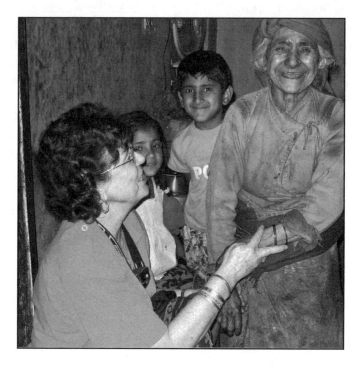

The old lady's smile tells it all

CHAPTER 30

A ONE-IN-TEN-BILLION CHANCE

තිංග්

E vil was watching keenly as two ladies started up a lonely forest trail in British Columbia, Canada. At the same time, a thousand miles away in Saskatchewan, Satan was hatching a plot to destroy a young family. In a one-in-ten-billion chance, the lives of this family were saved by a simple mistake.

Late one November, our friend Elizabeth Bovett came to visit us from Melbourne, Australia. After enjoying a relaxing time in Dallas, and a very pleasant Thanksgiving Day celebration together, Elizabeth flew up to Seattle, Washington. We had arranged for her to stay with our friends, Ervin and Adina Bergmann in Yarrow, British Columbia. She rented a car at the Seattle airport and drove up to Canada, having no idea that Evil was stalking her holiday path.

The plan was for Adina to show Elizabeth around the beautiful city of Victoria on Vancouver Island. However, there was a ferry strike pending on that very weekend.

Rather than risk getting stuck on the island, they decided to be safe and see the sights closer to home.

On Saturday, December 7th, just thirty minutes from Bergmanns' home, a robber had staked out a Cultus Lake parking lot. The two unsuspecting women arrived and parked Elizabeth's rental car from the U.S.A. The crook, no doubt, noticed that neither of them was carrying a purse or bag when they started up the trail to Tea Pot Mountain.

Two hours later, Elizabeth and Adina returned to find the driver's side window smashed. Their purses, which had been well hidden under the car seat, were gone. Cash, credit cards, drivers' licenses, and Elizabeth's Australian passport were all stolen. They immediately returned home and began canceling credit cards and phoning every place concerned about the loss. Even so, the thief had already charged $650 on Elizabeth's credit card.

Meanwhile, on the prairies of Canada a thousand miles to the East, a disaster was developing. It was a snowy winter's day and the gas furnace in a farmer's home had quit. He had called a repairman who had gotten it running again. However, unbeknown to them, the humidity and cold weather had combined to plug the exhaust pipe with ice and snow. Although the furnace was working again, undetectable fumes were now entering the house. As carbon monoxide stealthily displaced the oxygen in their bloodstream, a father and mother along with their children were quietly being overcome by the invisible poison.

The following Saturday, the Bergmanns noticed that their answering machine registered a call from Saskatchewan. Supposing it had to do with the Canadian

Sunday School Union, which Ervin represented, he returned the phone call a few days later. To his surprise, Ervin reached a farmer. In a somewhat embarrassed and shy manner the young man said, "I guess thanks are in order. If you had not phoned us, we would have died from carbon monoxide poisoning!" It was a short conversation, and Erv wished him a Merry Christmas.

Adina phoned back later and talked to the wife who gave her more information. Apparently, their phone had caller I.D. which had recorded a call from the Bergmanns. Adina then remembered that when she had been trying to contact a credit card office she had dialed a wrong number. This was about 8 p.m. and in Saskatchewan, two time zones to the east, it would have been 10 p.m. When an answering machine had clicked on, she realized it was a private home phone and had hung up. Those few rings of the phone, however, had roused the drowsy farmer enough for him to recognize that he and his family were being overcome by the lethal gas!

Now what are the odds of this happening? A long distance call requires a #1 plus ten numbers to be dialed. For each digit punched there is a choice of ten numbers. Everything else being equal, to randomly dial a particular wrong number, the odds are 10 x 10 x 10 x 10 x 10 x 10 x 10 x 10 x 10 x 10. That is, a one-in-ten-billion chance!

Consider the timing of that wrong-number call. It was after dinner when Adina suddenly remembered that she had failed to contact one credit card office. By that time, the family in Saskatchewan had already gone to bed. By this time, the poisoning process had progressed far enough for the farmer to know that something was disastrously wrong. Yet, it was soon enough that he could still be wakened from his stupor by a few rings of a telephone!

But Joseph said to them… 'You intended to harm me,
but God intended it for good to
accomplish what is now being done,
the saving of many lives.'
Genesis 50:19-20

—Postscript—

From the most ancient of times, a battle on earth has been raging between Good and Evil. In some cases, God prevails and Good obviously wins out. But in many instances, it is very apparent that Evil has had its way. In such cases, this apparent triumph of Evil becomes a test for us, and we can be left to wonder whether God cares or not. Experiences of this nature can be perplexing. They can leave us either bitter, or better... the choice is ours.

On rare occasions, however, God offers us the privilege of catching a glimpse of His intricate plan. He shows us how He has orchestrated a situation such as this to bring Good out of Evil... to the saving of many lives.

CHAPTER 31

BAJU'S BLESSING

ॐ∽ॐ

June 4, 1996

Tears streamed down Kerry's face as she turned away. "We'll never see Baju again Gary!" she predicted as we started up the long trail towards the mountain pass.

At eighty-four, Baju was the oldest man living in that part of the mountain range. The year before, he had so proudly told me how he too, had done his part in building the Magar Road that was to be known as Barbara's Highway. Sitting on the ground, his still powerful shoulders had methodically handled the axe. He had persevered for six days in the oppressive heat, cutting out huge, thick roots of a massive tree.

But now his health was obviously going downhill. With an infectious smile he thanked me and eagerly devoured the two bananas I offered him. But otherwise, he did not have the same appetite as before. His wife Kissery, of course, saw it more readily. She was upset that he would soon leave her and remarked, *"Baju cho, shike pamone."*

I was not one to readily accept her dire prediction that "Baju is trying to die." But she was right. Before we returned to Arakhala some months later, Baju had gone to be with his Lord.

Over the past twenty-three years, Baju had regularly picked up his crutches and headed out across the mountains on one leg to visit his old drinking buddies. Traveling from village to village, he would tell about the great peace and joy he had discovered when God had forgiven him of all his sins. Of course, sharing how he had asked Jesus to come into his heart and be the Lord of his life always put him at risk of insult and ridicule, not to mention the chance of being thrown into jail or worse.

One evening in Arakhala, Baju was sitting at the resting place beneath the enormous spreading banyan tree across from our house when the witchdoctor and his cronies surrounded him. It actually happened twice. On the first occasion, they threatened to kill him with their heavy sticks if he did not rejoin them in the village sacrifices. Baju's response was to unbutton his shirt, extend his neck as if he were to be sacrificed and say, "Go ahead. You can kill my body, but not my soul!"

They themselves were terrified of death, and this fearless response astonished them. Dumbfounded, they just stood there while Baju picked up his crutches and made his way through the crowd untouched. The incident seemed not unlike the account of what Jesus had done in Nazareth (Luke 4:28-30). On the second occasion, Baju called upon the witchdoctor's son to "poop right here." Again they were taken aback, and again he picked up his crutches and walked through their midst (See Chapter 29 of *Angel Tracks in the Himalayas*).

Now perhaps, Kissery was recalling that time Baju was in the Dhobari jail. How would she ever manage without him? For three hours, she had limped up the steep mountain. She had used every tactic she knew to persuade him to satisfy the police and get out of jail. But all of her tears had not moved him in the least. Baju was certain that God would look after them in all their circumstances. He steadfastly held to Jesus' teaching that those who seek to save their life will lose it (Luke 9:24).

He would do nothing to evade whatever punishment the Hindu government had in store for him for following Jesus. If God wanted him to get out of jail, He could do it… His way. But he was not going to give a single rupee to the police to somehow make it easier on himself. Noticing Kissery's limp, he prayed for her leg, and that evening she returned home walking normally.

On this trip to Arakhala, we had brought along a video camera to record various events in the village, and Baju did not seem to notice it in my hand. Before we parted, Baju, as usual, began to pray. It occurred to me that this would be a moment to remember, so I switched the camera on.

Baju's heart and soul reached up to heaven and Scriptures that were dear to his heart, words that he had put to the test over the past two decades, rolled off his tongue with compassion, power, and love. As he prayed for Kerry and me before we began yet another long journey, he concluded by blessing us saying, *May He give you the desire of your heart, and make all your plans succeed* (Psalm 20:4).

His words moved me so deeply that for just the second time in my life, I wrote a date beside the verse in my Bible: June 4, 1996.

—Postscript—

Baju could have included himself in that blessing, but it was so like him to center his thoughts on others first. Though he never saw his only son come to follow Jesus, Baju had seen a number of people do so in other villages across the mountains. He had only one child, a son. When his son had retired from the Indian Army, he had taken responsibility for their few small fields up on Peak-of-the-gods. There, not unlike his father before him, he drank often and drank much. His father-in-law was a witchdoctor, and he and his children preferred those ways rather than Baju's ways. After all, with the witchdoctor, there was no need for repentance, or a change of heart or lifestyle. Primarily, it just required lots of blood sacrifices.

But now, eleven years later, things have changed. Last night, as I talked on the phone with Peatam in Nepal, he told me about the wife of Baju's grandson. She had become sick and afflicted in several ways, and after six months of suffering was close to dying. She had gone down the mountain to her grandfather, the witchdoctor. He called upon all his spirit helpers, offered the sacrifices, and used every kind of magic he knew. Nevertheless, she was not healed. Finally, he told her to go back to Arakhala. "The Christians will heal you," he said.

She went up the mountain and asked Peatam and friends to pray for her. When they did, the power of the afflicting spirits was broken and she was healed. Although she is a granddaughter by marriage, it makes no difference. She is Baju's *khon*. She is the first of Baju's family to follow Jesus, and in due time her husband Mailha and others will likely follow as well.

CHAPTER 32

THE ESCAPE

෧෫෮

"**B**hee-sing! *Bhee-sing!* (Escape! Escape!)" Gyan kept saying to himself.

At the top of a ridge north of Arakhala sits the village of Danthok. In 1973, Baju began regularly going there to share the story of Jesus. His nephew Gyan was still a small boy then and he would stay the night at Gyan's house, even though no one paid much attention to his fervent message.

Now, eighteen years later, Gyan was trapped. He had lied, and there was no escape. He was a prisoner of his own making and there was no way out.

Baju had given money to help him attend college, and Haree had been so very kind to him. Every time he came to Kathmandu to get medicine for his sister, he had been warmly invited to stay in Haree's home. One day Haree asked him what he wanted to do with his life. Gyan replied that he wanted to go back to his village and share the story of Jesus. In fact, he had lied. He had no intention of doing that. Never mind though. He knew this was the answer that would most please Haree and Baju.

Consequently, Haree had been urging him repeatedly to take some Bible classes. To keep the lie going, Gyan had always agreed replying, "Of course, of course." But again, he had no intention of doing so whatsoever.

One day in July he came to Kathmandu to get more medicine for his epileptic sister, and as usual he stayed at Haree's place. The next thing he knew, Haree had filled out an application for the three-month long Discipleship Training Course. He signed it, and took Gyan to the YWAM base. Course supervisors, Mick and Mary, knew Haree well. And even though the course had started a week earlier, on Haree's recommendation they enrolled Gyan.

Haree was a forceful young man and one who got things done. He had supposed outright that Gyan was a genuine believer and he would pay no attention to any foot-dragging on Gyan's part. So here Gyan was, enrolled in this course. Day after day he was subjected to Bible study, prayer and practical Christian teaching. Oh, how he yearned to be free from it all! Week after week, Gyan kept wracking his brain, "Escape! How can I escape?"

His problem was that he was deeply indebted to both Haree and Baju. Furthermore, he was an "honest" person. He had never done anything wrong, so the message of God's forgiveness through Jesus held little interest for him. But if he ran away in the middle of this course, both Haree and Baju would realize that he had lied. They would know that he had deceived them. This would be so shameful, and how could he face them after that? Until he could come up with a reasonable excuse there was no escape.

God, however, had a plan. That plan included an escape for Gyan. After some two months, the course required a three-day session of prayer and private meditation. Even though he thought that such a good person as him really didn't need it, Gyan dutifully meditated and prayed.

During one of those sessions, God suddenly revealed Himself to Gyan. His eyes were opened to his pride, his selfishness, and his self-centeredness. He saw himself living in disgusting sin, particularly when compared to the standard Jesus set. He recognized the great magnitude of his sin, and realized he rightly deserved to be severely punished. Jesus, however, had freely taken that punishment for him. Jesus cared for him!

Gyan repented, and the relief he felt was palpable. He'd never known such peace. In the next few days, the presence of God amazed him, and he experienced incredible joy.

For all these weeks, he had focused only on escaping, and had looked everywhere to find a way out. Everywhere except to God. But now, God Himself had found him and had provided an escape. His Father had forged that escape route 2,000 years earlier. It set him free from the consequences of his pride and the selfishness that had blinded him to his separation from God. God, in fact, had now opened up for him the escape route to heaven, and was he glad!

And everyone who calls on the Name
of the Lord will be saved.
Acts 2:21

—Postscript—

Eventually, Gyan himself became a full-time worker with YWAM. When he saw that his parents would never grasp the Good News message unless he returned home, he did just that.

CHAPTER 33

REMEMBER

⮞⮜

Some faced jeers and flogging...
They were destitute, persecuted and mistreated—
the world was not worthy of them.
They wandered in deserts and mountains,
and in caves and in holes in the ground.
Hebrews 11:36-38

June 1999

I was about as upset as I could get. In fact, I was on the verge of becoming very angry. They had taken away a young man's teenage wife... possibly for good, because he had decided to follow Jesus.

Kerry and I were looking across the gorge that afternoon from Arakhala Village, and we could clearly see that cluster of houses clinging to a sharp ridge below Peak-of-the-gods. I knew I could reach that little village in less than three hours, and rescue Bir Bahadur and his young wife. If I delayed, they might beat him, or worse we feared, push him over a cliff.

But should I go? As Kerry and I discussed the situation, we were not sure what to do. How could we just stand aside and let this injustice, this travesty occur? How could we simply sit there and watch? On the other hand, we were foreigners and it was certainly not our practice to interfere with village affairs.

As usual, the key question boiled down to what would Jesus have us do? We had to hear from Him! Had God given Bir Bahadur unusual courage to go into that dark village alone? Or was Satan using this young man's foolish passions to lead him into a trap to destroy him?

Twenty-six years earlier, old Baju had begun making trips across the mountains with the express purpose of sharing the amazing story of Jesus Christ. Down the mountain and at the top of another steep ridge was the village of Danthok. There, Baju would often stop for the night and stay with one of his mother's relatives. Soon after he left, however, Gyan, the youngest son in the house, would regularly burn the Christian literature that he left with them.

Nevertheless, Baju persevered… never losing hope, never losing enthusiasm. Many years later, Gyan went on to college and became the most educated Magar in the area. Eventually, he became a believer and joined the work of YWAM.

A few years later, Gyan was assigned to his village area so he would have an opportunity to teach his parents. Meanwhile, his older sister had died, leaving a son who was being raised by Gyan's parents. This orphaned, illiterate teenage boy had become the village hoodlum.

Recently though, he had begun to listen and learn. Little by little, Gyan had taught his nephew, Bir Bahadur, to read the Magar New Testament. Eventually, he too believed, and carefully, but unashamedly shared the Good News.

In the course of things, Bir Bahadur married a sweet, shy girl from this village across the gorge from Arakhala. When Gyan's parents also became believers, it was the last straw for the leader of Danthok Village. These followers of Jesus destroyed the village harmony. They refused to pay their share for the sacrifices that placated the village gods! They were threatened over and over, and finally given an ultimatum: quit following Jesus or leave! They refused. They would neither forsake their God, nor abandon their home and village.

One day, they were handed a piece of paper to sign. In essence it meant that they would agree to follow the ways of their ancestors and pay their part for the village sacrifices. They refused to sign it.

That evening a crowd gathered. "Kill! Kill!" they shouted and began to beat them. So, the angry villagers drove them away in the dark of night with only the shirts on their backs. Twice Bir Bahadur went back to retrieve some essentials from their house. But before he could get his hands on anything, he was beaten and run off again. Since they could no longer return to their village, they settled into their little cattle shed an hour's walk below the ridge.

All might have been well if the ancestral spirits, the village gods and the demons had taken their fury out on these five traitors. But they didn't... or couldn't. Hence, the villagers thought that those spirits would hurt or kill

207

someone else in Danthok. Or, in their frustration, they might even wreak havoc upon the whole village.

Something had to be done about these Christians, and their adversaries had one more scheme. They went to the girl's father and prevailed upon him to help. In Magar culture, the father retains authority to annul a marriage until his daughter has given birth to a child. In a Hindu nation where women and girls are sometimes treated no better than slaves, this provision in Magar culture gives them a significant level of protection.

If the father feels that his daughter is not being cared for properly, he can take her back home and end the marriage. In such a case, the father's decision is law. This custom may not be so widely known. However, I well remember the day in Arakhala many years earlier when Baju's brother Gopal did just that and retrieved his daughter from her new husband's home. That was the end of it, and there was no controversy whatsoever. Some time later she married someone else.

So it was that Bir Bahadur received an invitation from his father-in-law to come up for a visit. He and his wife knew, however, what that invitation meant, so they did not go. They knew that their decision stood against Magar customs and it would surely strain the relationship. The invitation came again, and yet again, but still they did not go. Subsequently, one day father arrived to take his daughter home. As an illiterate, very pregnant, teenage girl she didn't know what to do except to obey her father.

Gyan was gone at the time, so immediately Peatam rushed down the mountain to support Bir Bahadur who wanted to rescue her and bring her back. But in that isolated mountain village, no one could assure his safety.

Peatam begged him to stay away for he knew they would force Bir Bahadur to deny Jesus.

If he refused to recant, they might beat him mercilessly. Or, even worse, he might "accidentally" slip off a cliff and that would solve their problem! If he must go, at least let a couple of the Christians accompany him, Peatam counseled. Perhaps their presence might afford him some protection.

A few days later, news came up the mountain that Bir Bahadur had gone to fetch his bride by himself. With absolutely no status, no authority, and no position from which to negotiate, this destitute, unschooled teenager and his young wife had no chance to prevail against a community's will.

On the day of his arrival, Father-in-law welcomed him warmly. The second day, Father-in-law began to insist that he return to the religion of their ancestors. On the third day he gave an ultimatum: "Make your choice! Choose your wife, or choose your Lord!"

Her father, as well as all the villagers certainly expected the young man to choose his pregnant wife. This wretched fellow had virtually nothing else on earth but her. How could he reject the love and only comfort in his life? And how could he forfeit his first child as well? Furthermore, if he lost her, who else would ever want to marry him?

Indeed, as they had anticipated, Bir Bahadur chose his wife and replied saying, "I cannot live without my wife."

But then he added, "And... I cannot live without my Lord!"

The villagers could never have imagined that a penniless, unlearned person from the dregs of Magar society would have a Friend in the highest. One, who at that very moment stood before God in heaven interceding on behalf of this miserable fellow. As Job had said, *My intercessor is my friend...on behalf of a man he pleads with God as a man pleads for his friend* (Job16:20-21).

They had given him an either-or proposition. But they were unprepared to deal with the wisdom of the ages that proceeded from his mouth when he chose both his wife *and* Jesus. This double-barreled answer confounded Father-in-law and he blurted out, "Well then, take her!"

Before anyone could have a second thought, they were out of the village and racing down the mountain to their little hovel at the cattle shed.

A couple of months later, Gyan was back at the cowshed where his family was living. One day, when he and his friend Kheman heard a call for help from the nearby corn field, they went to investigate. Bir Bahadur's wife had given birth to a baby girl. After deep thought sometime later, Uncle Gyan proposed a name for the baby. "Call her *Sum-jhana*, (Remembrance)" he said.

He had thought, "May this child be a remembrance of the faith and courage of her father and mother. Seeing her, may everyone remember how our God on High put the right words into her father's mouth."

And so, Remembrance lives today as a testimony to the love and compassionate care of their Friend, who preserved her family even before she was born.

Remember how the
LORD your God led you all the way
in the desert these forty years.
Deuteronomy 8:2

—Postscript—

In retrospect, it is clear how close I came to interfering with God's plan. I could have ruined that day… a day of bold courage and high faith which has become a part of Sum-jhana's family history. I would have ruined the opportunity for Bir Bahadur to exhibit this watershed incident of overcoming faith.

I could have rescued his wife and saved Bir Bahadur from the threat of bodily harm. But surely, this would not have produced reconciliation with his father-in-law. In fact, by interfering I would have embarrassed Father-in-law and could have antagonized him further. And, had he wanted to, the very next day he could have taken his daughter back again and there would have been no way that I could have prevented it. This time, however, we had done the right thing. We had prayed for Bir Bahadur and settled our wavering trust on the loving care of God. Clearly, that was God's plan.

Sometimes, just trusting God is enough.

—Peatam – Baju's Disciple—

(1995-2003)

❧

CHAPTER 34

THREE SHAMANS

ತಿಂ

*The steps of a good man are
ordered by the Lord.*
Psalms 37:23

Peetam was amazed. Here were three shamans, all
sitting in the same small room, all working together.
This kind of cooperation was unheard of in this mountain
area.

Darkness had fallen by the time Peatam and Kumari
arrived on one of those somewhat irregular, bi-monthly
trips over the mountains to Kumari's village. Years earlier
they had learned that God would arrange divine
appointments for them, so they had come to expect the
unexpected. And once again, so it was this evening… this
time, as soon as they reached the village.

Before they had even gotten to Kumari's home, they
came across a house that was surrounded by people. In
fact, there were probably sixty people pressing around the
little door, packed in together like a swarm of bees. When
they inquired about what was happening, they

immediately understood. They knew why they had arrived on this day, at just this time.

Praying as they went, Peatam and Kumari squeezed and pushed their way through the crowd and in the narrow door. Once inside the little house, they discovered three shamans sitting around a fire, each holding the burnt stub of a grass broom. All day long they had been lighting one strand after another of their brooms and blowing the fire and smoke onto their patient. Despite their incantations and mantras, their best efforts had been futile.

The victim, they discovered, turned out to be Kumari's thirty-year-old aunt. She, as well as the shamans, were completely covered with ashes. Earlier, others reported, she had been thrashing around uncontrollably, but now she lay motionless before them on the ground. One might have supposed she was dead.

If not exhausted, the shamans were certainly frustrated by the futility of their day-long efforts. So when Peatam arrived, they promptly offered him the opportunity to see what he could do. He and Kumari simply put their hands on Aunty and prayed a short prayer in Jesus' name. Aunty immediately sat up and began talking. Not only did she talk, she was also in her right mind. To test whether she was actually okay, others asked her to identify Peatam and Kumari, which she readily did.

Now to Him who is able to do immeasurably more
than all we ask or imagine, according to
His power that is at work within us...
Ephesians 3:20

—Postscript—

Shamans gain the cooperation of powerful familiar spirits and are widely feared. Thus, they hold a position of influence and power in their villages. Because they can profit nicely from their trade, they often compete fiercely with one another. Why these three had teamed together to try to bring about a deliverance, Peatam never learned.

From this time onward, whenever Peatam saw a shaman in the village, he would detect a look of alarm come upon the man's face. They knew he was not a shaman and did not realize it was the power of Jesus that did the healing. So they could only suppose that he must be a *boksa*, a male witch. But what sort of major spirit powers did he control to have performed such a spectacular miracle so effortlessly? In their religious system, they were rightfully terrified. One day, they assumed, he might curse them with a mighty demon spirit that would make them crazy and drive them to a dreadful death.

They didn't understand, of course, Peatam's desire that they be freed from their bondages and fear. They didn't know that in Jesus' kingdom, His followers did not use black magic and curses to obtain power. They didn't realize that there should be no competition. They had no idea that just as God loved them they were to love and care for one another.

CHAPTER 35

THE LION ATTACK
∂∾∽

Your enemy the devil prowls around like a
roaring lion looking for someone to devour.
1 Peter 5:8

June 1999

A lion looking for prey crouched at the edge of
Kumari's village. When he burst from the forest
with a terrifying roar, Peatam was all but paralyzed with
fear.

The massive animal with great flowing mane had its
eyes fixed on him, and Peatam was going to be its dinner!
He could clearly count every tooth in its gaping mouth,
and its enormous white fangs were as long as his fingers!
With swift, determined strides it would close the thirty
yards between them in a moment.

Where would he run? Where might he hide?

Deep in his spirit, however, Peatam understood he
must stand his ground! This was not the time to run. Now

was not the time for hiding. Though he was so puny compared to this great beast, still he must fight!

Peatam turned sideways, and as a policeman halting traffic might do, stretched forth his hand. As one aiming a gun, he looked down his arm staring directly at the huge lion bearing down upon him.

More than ever before, this was the time to steadfastly "lean-his-heart" upon Father God, his Creator. It was the time to call upon Jesus.

Just the previous evening, after a long, tiring journey Peatam and Kumari had reached Kumari's home village of Dant Besi. That night, Kumari's mother had told them that they needed to see Uncle Sailha immediately. He was so desperately ill that he might be dead before morning.

Some months earlier, Uncle had taken sick. He had gone to the witchdoctors, but the sacrifices of goats and chickens had not helped. Then, though he had little money, he went to the Tansen Mission Hospital, as well as to three other government hospitals. The results were no better. Subsequently, his face darkened and his body wasted away until his skin was just draped over bare bones.

For the past three months he had been unable to walk... paralyzed from the waist down. In the early hours before dawn, he would shriek and cry out, tormented by excruciating pain. The moment those dreadful attacks came upon him, everyone in the village heard it.

That night Peatam and Kumari climbed up on top of the chicken pen. They rolled out a thin rice-straw mat over some rough boards and lay down. Then they prayed, "Lord Jesus, we are going to sleep now. Tonight and tomorrow look after Uncle Sailha. Show him your great power."

The Lion Attack

They fell asleep that night, trusting in their Great God of compassion and might. They understood better than most that this problem could only be solved by their Father in heaven. But now, the lion had arrived. He was hungry and looking for someone to devour.

The advance was rapid. The attack was quick. Within seconds it was all over.

As Peatam stood his ground, calling upon that Name above all names, the lion began to shrink. This did not slow its determined attack and he kept right on coming. With each step the animal took, however, the smaller it became.

By the time the terrifying beast leaped upon him, the lion had become a tiny miniature of its former self. Peatam grabbed it, and his hands closed around its body. With a twist and a jerk, he showed me how he had torn the lion's head off and thrown the two pieces to the ground.

At dawn the next morning, Peatam and Kumari left for Uncle's village. It was a full hour's climb up the steep mountain trail. With each step they praised God for this answer to their prayers. They were certain of the interpretation of Peatam's dream. God had called them to stand in the gap for Uncle, and they knew beyond all doubt that Satan had been defeated.

When they arrived at the village, an old grandmother a few houses away called out to them. "Did Uncle die last night?" she inquired.

After all, for the first time in three months, she had not been awakened in the early morning darkness by his blood-curdling screams. That comment only confirmed what they had been so confident of in their hearts. They would pray, and Uncle would not only be delivered from the Evil One, he would also be restored to life and health. Of this they were certain.

—Postscript—

When I quizzed Peatam further about his dream, he assured me that he had been attacked by a lion, an animal native to a region in next door India. The animal was not a *chituwa*, a leopard. Neither was it a *rang-ghu*, a tiger. It was a *gaja-kesari*, a lion!

The believers in Arakhala are very aware of the spiritual warfare that constantly goes on around them. Paul's admonition to put on the armor of God is an important part in this battle (Ephesians 6:10 -18). When Peatam demonstrated for me how he had faced this fearsome attack, the spiritual imagery was clear. His outstretched arm was holding firmly to an invisible shield of faith.

Then there was the sword of the Spirit, which is the Word of God. Boldly he spoke forth the name of that One who is called the Word: Jesus, the One who is God our Savior, the King of kings, and Lord of lords. The One who had prayed, *Holy Father, protect them by the power of Your name—the name You gave me* (John 17:11).

This lion was not pouncing upon just another hapless victim. Instead, he was confronted by an all-powerful shield of faith. Slashed by the sword of the Word, Satan's terrifying power was destroyed. Much like a balloon that has been pierced, that enormous predator swiftly shrank to almost nothing.

Peatam had no physical ability whatsoever to stand against that lion. But because Jesus lived in him, because he had put on the armor of Christ, he knew in his spirit that he had all that was necessary to overcome. Because Peatam trusted Him implicitly, Jesus became both his strength and his shield. He knew Jesus had said, *All authority in heaven and on earth has been given to me.* (Matthew 28:18). Armed with the authority that Jesus had promised him, Peatam stood his ground in the battle.

As for Uncle, his recovery came about in three stages. That day, Peatam took some oil and massaged his back. He prayed for God to heal his back and take away the pain. That, he stated, was all the faith I had at the time. A month later they returned and found Uncle stronger and without pain. This time they prayed for God to give strength to his legs so he could move around.

After another month they returned again and found Uncle outside his house, but leaning heavily on a stick. Peatam put oil on him a third time and prayed for God to give him strength to be able to work productively. Indeed, over time his health was fully restored. Today, he once again carries heavy loads across the mountains. Nevertheless, spiritual darkness maintains an iron grip on that mountain region east of Arakhala. Consequently, Uncle has been unable to comprehend the great spiritual freedom he would experience by entrusting his life to Jesus. Disrupting the harmony of village life by following a "foreign god" would bring too much shame upon his family. To date, he seems unable to break with the traditions of his ancestors.

CHAPTER 36

BAPTIZED 101 TIMES

ॐ

For our light and momentary troubles are achieving for us an eternal glory that far outweighs them all. So we fix our eyes not on what is seen, but on what is unseen. For what is seen is temporary, but what is unseen is eternal.
2 Corinthians 4:17-18

Beaten again and again, Lata steadfastly refused to submit. His mother had just died, and Hindus will not compromise when it comes to observing their death ceremonies. When he refused to perform those rituals, they would have none of it.

Lata is from Chainpur, a small village on the ridge just west of Arakhala. His name indicates his condition. He is deaf and dumb. Lata is not a Magar, but rather a low-caste blacksmith. His older brother has much the same disabilities, though he can speak a little and hear somewhat.

Peatam has befriended Lata, and with gestures and hand signs they communicate quite well. In Arakhala

Village, Peatam is his closest friend. Some years ago, Lata became a follower of Jesus. Later, he publicly showed his allegiance to Jesus by being baptized. For that decision, he endured considerable persecution, but the worst was yet to come.

Two important parts of the Hindu funeral ceremony are a ritual dipping in the river and shaving one's head. When Lata wouldn't do that, the villagers dragged him down the mountain to the Kali Gandaki River. Holding him down, they shaved all the hair off his head, including his eyebrows. Then they took him into the river and pushed him under the water. By forcing these rituals upon him they presumed that he would be defiled and consequently rejected both by Jesus and the Christians. "There," they thought, "Lata is now a Hindu again."

When he came up from the water they asked him if he would recant. He wouldn't, so they beat him some more and pushed him under the water again. The villagers were certain that they could persuade this stupid, cursed man, and they were determined to overcome his stubbornness. Lata, however, stood his ground.

The headwaters of the Kali Gandaki originate on the Tibetan plateau north of the Himalayas. Since this was December, the water was freezing cold. Again they beat him and pushed him under. Again, Lata refused to deny Jesus.

Now they began counting. How many times would it take to change his mind? On they went... ten... twenty... thirty times! Still they beat Lata, and still he refused. When they finally reached one hundred baptisms, they quit. It appeared that he would rather die than alter his resolve.

Though Lata is dirt-poor and has a rough life, he clearly understands his physical challenges are only temporary. As a result, he seems contented with the state that he has found himself in. He knows that in eternity his spirit will occupy a perfect heavenly body that is free of life's earthly sorrows.

He will wipe every tear from their eyes.
There will be no more death or mourning
or crying or pain, for the old order
of things has passed away.
Revelation 21:4

—Postscript—

Some time later, Lata was visiting another village. There, he discovered that the pastor's wife was continuing to worship her Hindu idols. He was incredulous that no one had been successful in clearly presenting the Good News message to her.

In Nepal, some deaf and dumb people communicate just marginally. Lata, however, is quite good, and interpreting his gestures is not particularly difficult. He told her of Jesus' death for us, and how He wanted to become our friend and take us to heaven to be with Him forever. Yes, life would be hard for the present, and he had experienced more difficulties than most. But in heaven, we would be free from it all. If, however, she went to hell, and he gestured as if he was lighting a fire, it would only be burning for her!

The problem with Lata was that once he had set his mind on something, it was most difficult to dissuade him.

Perseverance was second nature to him. Furthermore, for someone who is deaf, you can yell your lungs out, but still he will not get the point. One day, God answered Lata's persistence and his heart's desire, and the pastor's wife, too, decided to follow Jesus.

He will respond to the prayer of the destitute;
He will not despise their plea.
Psalm 102:17

Peatam and Kumari
(Peatam was one of Michael's childhood friends)

CHAPTER 37

A MOST UNUSUAL MIRACLE
ન્છેન્જી

P eatam and Kumari had good reason to be discouraged. Despite their innumerable trips to her home village, response to the Good News was nil. Of course the Magar people appreciated their love and caring attitudes, and they were grateful for the healings and deliverances that relieved them of so much suffering. However, that was where it all ended.

Now, Kumari's thirty-one year old Aunt was sick again. This time it was a terrible fever, and she was no longer making any sense when she talked. The family had acquired some medicine for her somewhere, but it had not helped. The shamans had already demonstrated their poor success in the healing arts the previous year. So the family felt that there was no reason to spend any more money on sacrifices and shamans in the faint hope that they might heal her now.

Mother-in-law, it seems, had learned that Peatam and Kumari had just arrived at Dant Besi Village. She had hope in them, and she was insistent that they be called. So at her request, a message was sent and the two agreed to make the short, thirty-minute walk over to Bhagar Village.

As was their habit, the couple prayed as they walked the trail. They did this particularly when they were called to pray for someone who was in desperate need. As before, they fully expected that God would make His presence known. But they wondered, would there be any long-term change in the villagers' attitudes or lives? Or would they continue to placate the gods and ancestral spirits with blood sacrifices in order to gain their favor and protection?

What they felt they needed, Peatam told me, was a miracle of unusual proportions. They did not presume to know what that might be, but nevertheless they boldly and concisely prayed, "Dear Lord, Aunty is too sick to even recognize her children anymore. Show her Your great power."

When they arrived at Bhagar Village, they did not know it, but Aunty was in an inner room of the house with a family member looking after her. Lying there on the floor, apparently unconscious, she suddenly sat straight up.

Less than a minute later, Peatam and Kumari entered the room. To them, Aunty did not look sick at all. In fact, she stood up and appeared normal and lucid. Peatam recalled that they could easily have believed that everyone had been lying about Aunty being so seriously ill. Like Peter's mother-in-law whom Jesus healed, she would have been quite able to fix them dinner, if it had been the time to do so (Matthew 8:14-17).

—Postscript—

The testimony of the lady attending Aunty affirmed that at the very moment Peatam and Kumari's feet touched their front yard, Aunty was completely healed. This healing occurred a year after her deliverance from demon powers. At the time of this writing no one has changed their allegiance and decided to follow Jesus. Perhaps they assume it is their karma, their good works in a previous incarnation that has earned them this unusual touch from God.

...enable your servants to speak
your word with great boldness.
Stretch out your hand to heal and perform
miraculous signs and wonders through
the Name of your holy servant Jesus.
Acts 4:29-30

CHAPTER 38

THE AUTHORITY OF JESUS

෧෧෧

Has not God chosen those who are poor in the
eyes of the world to be rich in faith?
James 2:5

P eatam had suffered for weeks with typhoid and
Kumari from some other illness. Summer was
ending and still they had not recovered their former
strength. Nevertheless, once the monsoon rains subsided,
they made another trip to her home village. When I was
young and strong, this would have been a vigorous eight-
hour trek for me.

It was a festival time, and they went with the express
purpose of being a light in that village with seven
shamans. The very next day, Kumari's village was
hosting a volleyball tournament, and about seventy young
men from nearby villages came to compete.

Kumari's uncle, Kailha, was playing for the home
team. When it came time for them to compete, Kailha
rolled up his wallet in his long pants and put them aside.
After the game was over he put his pants back on only to

discover that his wallet had disappeared. It was impossible for it to have just fallen out, so he raised an outcry.

His fellow players began to search everyone's pockets and eventually it was found. The thief, however, claimed that the wallet was his, and a big argument ensued. In the end, the thief could not substantiate his story and was forced to give it back. This incident brought great shame, not only upon him, but upon his village as well.

One of the men on the thief's volleyball team was a powerful shaman. In retaliation for the humiliation, he "shot" Kailha with a curse. Uncle had no defense against the curse, and he was overpowered by a powerful demon spirit. Immediately, he went totally crazy.

In the villages, shamans are relied upon to help those attacked by evil spirits, but in fact, not uncommonly they use their spirit helpers to intimidate or retaliate. In this case, the victim went completely wild and Uncle began beating people up. In fact, he became so powerful that no one could subdue him. Peatam recounted that it reminded him of the demons that Jesus encountered in the Gerasene demoniac (Mark 5:1-20).

Since Uncle was uncontrollable, someone went off to find Peatam and Kumari, whose God was known to have power over the demons. After a twenty-minute walk around the ridge, the two arrived to find the man raging violently. Upon seeing Peatam and Kumari, however, the demon immediately went quiet. Walking over to Uncle, they began commanding the spirit to leave. Peatam recounted how surprised they were when they did not have to shout and demand that the demon obey them. With seemingly little resistance, it left.

—Postscript—

This sort of happening may be unfamiliar ground for some, but not for the uncomplicated people I am familiar with in Asia. The lives they live, and the faith they practice is much more akin to that found in the New Testament than to that which is generally known in America.

For our short time here on earth, we humans are essentially spirit beings who have been confined to human flesh... *clay pots*, as the Apostle Paul describes our bodies. As for Peatam and Kumari, perhaps this demon clearly saw Jesus in them. Maybe it recognized that they had hearts and minds united to sacrificially serve the Father, His creation, and His son, Jesus.

Though both had been wronged countless times, they had learned to readily and freely forgive each and every person. In addition, they were free of such habits as criticism, envy, and pride and this fortified the doorways to their minds. Consequently, this demon knew he could not successfully bombard them with thoughts of shame, worry, and fear. When commanded in the name of Jesus, it left immediately and went elsewhere in search of better pastures.

And these signs will accompany those who believe:
In my Name they will drive out demons.
Mark 16:17

—More of God's Astonishing—
Power

❧❧

CHAPTER 39

FLYING HIGH

ᘒᙄ

North Pacific—39,000 feet
January 30, 2004

Dearest Cammie,

We're fighting a bit of headwind tonight. That is pretty regular for this time of winter. When we left Los Angeles it was midnight, so on this leg of our trip we are traveling in darkness all the way. Now, after nine hours in the air, we are flying over Japan and expect to land in Taipei in another five hours.

This week we were very surprised and really disappointed to learn that the chemo for your cancer is no longer working. So, while I'm thinking about it, I wanted to put down a few thoughts about what you and I will soon experience.

I say soon, since in Psalm 90:4 we are reminded that in heaven a day is as a thousand years. By my calculation, that computes to about one hour for every forty years. So, to use the word "soon" to describe an hour or two in heaven seems reasonable to me.

As our body weakens, flesh and blood lose their power to insulate our spirit from the presence of heaven. That, perhaps, is surprisingly good news!

At some point in this process, you will naturally wonder about what is going to happen to those people and to those things that mean the most to you. You may suppose that if your body only had more strength, and if it would just hold together a little while longer that you could have a greater impact on this world. It is right and good to think this way... to have our lives focused on giving and on making an impact for God's Kingdom. However, on the other side of the coin, our few days here on earth are nothing more than an apprenticeship to prepare us for eternity.

I remember those questions I had sixteen years ago as clearly as if it were happening right now. There was no hope that I would live. It was not even a consideration. When the rifle bullet struck the front of my belt and exploded out my back, a cantaloupe-size chunk of intestines, muscle, and pelvis were ripped to shreds.

Driving at top speed for medical help was doing the right thing. But I knew... I knew that their efforts were purely for show. The doors of heaven were already swinging open.

As the powerful Dodge pickup roared up onto Interstate Highway 10, three things came to my mind... those things I cared for most in life: (1) my wife, Barbara, (2) my children, Adina and Michael, and (3) the Magars and the Magar New Testament translation. Who would take care of them? What would their future be without me?

We were the only ones who had learned the Magar language and culture, investing over eighteen years in it.

Who would ever finish the New Testament for over half a million Magars... and when? As rapidly as those concerns formed in my mind, Jesus spoke so clearly to my heart, "I will! I've got it covered!"

Well, with that taken care of, I was out of here. If Jesus was going to take responsibility for it all, then I was free to go.

The Emergency Room nurses at the Kerrville Hospital waited for the DOA; that is, the man who would be "dead on arrival." Meanwhile, I waited patiently for the angels and the open door to appear. I waited, and waited, and waited. I waited eagerly, expectantly... the peace and presence of God so thick, so strong. No strength remained in my body; my earthly life was hanging by a single breath. There was so little now... just the thinnest of veils separating my spirit from the very sight of God. I knew. I could feel it... I just couldn't see Him yet.

Then, forty-eight hours later, a nurse unhooked a couple of contraptions, and I began to sense it. Something terrible was happening! I had turned a corner. If I had had any strength left, I would have wept bitterly.

Yes, I had missed my promotion. It had been ripped out of my very grasp. The open door to heaven had suddenly slammed closed! My body was beginning to rally now, and as my flesh thickened around my spirit's senses, God's tangible presence was being crowded out. Desperately I wanted to scream out, "Noooooooo!"

Later, I wondered in amazement at the complete absence of fear I had experienced. For forty-six years the world had taught me that dying was to be feared. But just as Jesus had described in John 5:24, my spirit had indeed crossed over from death into life... way back on January 2, 1965. And as my flesh was losing its strength, my spirit was finally acquiring unfettered freedom. My soul already had eternal life in Christ, and there was not a thing to be feared about leaving my flesh behind. My spirit recognized this, and my body had suddenly become unnecessary baggage.

Paul writes about it this way. *Though outwardly we are wasting away, yet inwardly we (our spirit-man) are being renewed more and more each day* (2 Corinthians 4:16).

And a bit later he writes about it again. *For while we are in this tent, we groan and are burdened, because we do not wish to be unclothed but to be clothed with our heavenly dwelling, so that what is mortal may be swallowed up by life* (2 Corinthians 5:4).

What I'm trying to describe is that when my flesh faded in strength, *life*, not death was swallowing it. Spirit-life had become supreme, and it was all part of God's great, unspeakable love to swallow up what was mortal.

None of us can say what the next day will bring. It's like when I have been body surfing in the ocean, no one can predict whether we will ride the first good wave all the way into the beach… or whether we will get sucked back out to sea, only to try another wave, and maybe another. We may have some assumptions based upon our experience and knowledge in this world. But we would do better to walk confidently with Jesus, knowing like King David that each of our days were written in God's book before one of them came to be (Psalm 139:16).

In any event, this is the sort of thing I expect you to experience when your body weakens. That veil will thin and your spirit will begin to know the presence of heaven. Some will understand. Others, however, will want to keep you and might implore you to hold onto life. But as for me, I'm out of here the moment Jesus tells me, "I've got it all covered."

Then, for the next couple of hours, from time to time I suppose, I'll slip over to the grandstand seats to watch those I care about most, and pray unhindered for them until they finish the race.

Blessing & Peace,
Uncle Gary

—Postscript—

Our dear friend, Cammie Jarvis, gave us permission to share my letter and her story.

When this letter was written, we had no surety that we would ever see her again this side of heaven. Cancer had ravaged her body for the third time and no more radiation or chemo treatments were available. Over a period of twenty years, she underwent fourteen major operations. The last two operations took out two-thirds of her right lung and three ribs. With all hope gone, the doctors suggested that her parents prepare themselves for the inevitable.

Eight weeks after her last operation, Cammie and her mother drove down to Houston, Texas, and attended a Healing Conference led by Charles and Frances Hunter. At some point, an invitation to come forward was given for those who wanted healing for cancer. Cammie did. When Frances prayed for her, Cammie didn't feel anything spectacular. However, she did feel a great peace and comfort come over her, coupled with a soaring faith that God had healed her.

Her mother told us that at that moment, she felt as if she were in the very presence of Jesus, presenting her dying daughter to Him. Though she herself had no assurance that Cammie would be healed, nevertheless, it was the most impacting experience she has ever known.

In fact, Cammie recovered miraculously. On her 28th birthday, June 9, 2007, with great thankfulness to God, we were in Dallas, Texas, to joyfully celebrate Cammie's marriage to Jeremy Jarvis! She has set aside her MA program and is teaching Special Needs children. Jeremy is occupied full-time with The Prayer Room ministry in Arlington, Texas.

CHAPTER 40

ALIVE FROM THE DEAD
ॐ

*For it has been granted to you on behalf
of Christ not only to believe on Him,
but also to suffer for Him.*
Philippians 1:29

The young man from the Tamang tribe was just my age. He had lived high in the Himalayas of Central Nepal, where life was basic, rugged, and simple. However, in 1968 a small booklet about Jesus found its way into his remote village, and his uncomplicated life changed dramatically.

This booklet told an exceptionally strange tale. In fact, it was so extraordinary that Bhim felt compelled to investigate it further. As a result, he made a hard, three-day journey out across the rough, jagged mountains to the little town of Pokhara. There he learned more, acquired a Nepali New Testament and returned home.

In the ensuing days and weeks, Bhim was overjoyed as he came to realize that all his sins were forgiven...

every single one! Furthermore, he was beginning to hear from God. This was a world apart from anything he had previously known. Beforehand, he always offered sacrifices to the mountain gods, the idols, and ancestral spirits. He could never be sure, however, if the blood of one animal was sufficient, so he and his people lived in constant fear of attack from those fickle, and often malevolent spirits.

Like Baju, Darima, and many others we have known, Bhim just couldn't contain himself. The more he learned, the more he shared. Before long, his wife, as well as a number of his village friends had begun to follow Jesus. Inevitably, though, the shaman and his cronies would have none of it.

They bullied. They harassed. They threatened and did all they knew to stop him. That, however, did not faze Bhim. He had a Friend now… a Friend who had promised never to leave him. He had a companion, the Son of the Living God. It was a tangible friendship he could never give up. But before long, Bhim was to experience more of the Scriptures than he might have understood. Jesus had stated, *The thief comes only to steal and kill and destroy* (John 10:10). In Bhim's case, Satan was to do it nearly all at once.

Like the Pharisees in Jesus' time, the shaman and his friends soon realized that there was but one solution to their problem. Accordingly, they attacked Bhim and tied him up hand and foot, and dragged the shameless rebel around the village like a sack of potatoes. When they reached the village center, they began to beat him brutally. The gang of men were worked into such a frenzy that no one dared interfere. They struck him viciously, and when he was dead they left his bloody, battered body where it lay.

The scene was similar, no doubt, to the Bible report of the stoning of Paul in Acts 14:19. After the mob had dispersed, Bhim's family carried his gruesome form back home. About four hours later, however, someone noticed that he had begun to breathe again... all but imperceptibly at first. And the next day, to everyone's astonishment, he regained consciousness. In fact, even more remarkable, in the following weeks he essentially recovered from the cruel beating.

The village shaman, however, wasn't finished. The next thing he did was to demand that all the troublemakers abandon their allegiance to Jesus Christ. Six families refused. These were forced to desert their houses and lands, and move out. As a result, Bhim left his Himalayan home and migrated down to the hot plains where he built a small hut for his family.

But Bhim couldn't simply settle down and quietly live out the rest of his life. He was deeply concerned for his friends who had recanted. They had just begun to follow Jesus. They understood so little and he felt compelled to do something about it. So at festival times, he would make the grueling trip back over the mountains to his Himalayan village, staying vigilant to keep out of sight.

At nighttime, he would quietly teach those who had been forced to abandon their faith. One time, however, he was seen and his visit reported to his adversaries. Subsequently, they sent someone to discover when he planned to return again. On the expected day several months later, they gathered to ambush him in the thick forest below the village. This time, they would finish him off once and for all!

On that mountainside, there is just one main trail into the village. As with most villages, there are a number of small paths that crisscross the mountain and lead out to fields, animal sheds, and little herdsmen's shelters. The next time Bhim came, he decided to take a small upper trail into the village where he hoped to visit someone along the way. This little path led him around the forest.

When the shaman and his friends discovered that he had taken the upper trail, they were certain that they had learned Bhim's strategy. The next time he returned, they gathered to ambush him there, but on that day he took a circuitous, lower trail to visit an uncle. This scenario was to repeat itself over and over again. Bhim later learned that the shaman eventually grew convinced that someone in their midst was secretly warning him.

At night in the village, the little homes were usually lit by a smoky wick that hung over the side of a small shallow clay bowl filled with mustard oil. It produced about as much light as a poor candle. The home where he stayed was secured on the inside with a strong wooden crossbar placed across the back of the only door. After everyone in the village had gone to sleep, Bhim would begin his underground meetings.

One time, about midnight, their worries became a reality. Bhim was whispering quietly as he taught the underground believers when someone arrived outside the door and called his name. A chill ran down his spine. He had been discovered!

The visitor reported that one of the Christians' chief persecutors lay dying, and he wanted Bhim to come and pray for him. Bhim knew, of course, that it was a trap. On no account would he be so foolish as to venture out in the dead of night.

He himself never spoke a word. Instead, the man of the house answered and sent the messenger away. Before long, the man returned and was rejected once more. Soon, the messenger returned yet again. The shamans had done all their sacrifices, all their magic and mantras, but now their man was breathing his last... so he said.

On no account would Bhim be so foolish, and they sent him away. The scheming rascals, persistent and now desperate ordered the messenger to go back yet again. So he returned and pleaded for Bhim to come and pray.

This time, Bhim had a clever idea. He would put an end to their nonsense. They told the messenger that Bhim would come and pray for the man on one condition. Before he prayed, every one of them would have to take a solemn oath to become followers of the Way, if Jesus healed their friend! That, Bhim was certain, would put an end to it. The messenger left, but, to their surprise, returned yet again. Yes, he reported, their adversary, as well as all of his companions, had agreed to this stipulation.

What?! That was impossible!

Bhim was in a dreadful predicament now. He had promised that he would go... if they would agree. But who would ever trust these people, particularly in the middle of the night? Unquestionably, he felt, it was all a lie. It was all just a trap to kill him. His friends were no help—not one had the courage to accompany him out into the darkness.

Bhim had never expected it to come to this. But how could he live with himself now? He had given his word. How could he face his people and proclaim the Truth... after they all learned that he had lied? It was a dreadful predicament.

Committing his soul into the hands of Jesus, he opened the creaky little door, and with fear and trepidation stepped out into the black night... alone. Just he and God. Bhim was deliberately walking straight into the presence of the same vicious mob that had once killed him... only because he had promised.

When he arrived at the man's house, it was just as the messenger had reported. Yes, indeed, they wanted him to pray! They had heard and seen that Jesus answered prayers. They had no hope left for their friend now, and he was obviously in his last hour of life.

Before proceeding, Bhim demanded that each and every one of them take a solemn oath. They must swear to follow Jesus if their comrade recovered. (Perhaps the Tamang custom is the same as the Magars'. If so, they might have stated, "I will follow Jesus. I will follow Jesus. I will follow Jesus!" Alternatively they could have said, "I will follow Jesus. One! Two! Three!"

To Bhim's great surprise, everyone did. Then he put his hand on the man and prayed. When he was finished, he turned and hurried back to his friend's house, exceedingly relieved to still be alive and well.

The next morning the dying man was still breathing. Then slowly, ever so slowly, he began to improve. After some months, he essentially recovered. As a result, most of the villagers discarded their idols and began to follow in the ways of Jesus.

As Bhim told me this account, it was vividly apparent how much his commitment to Jesus had cost him. During the telling, he often paused as he struggled to gain control of his emotions and tears. Then softly, and with difficulty, he would recall the rejection, the fears, the beating, the pain and persecution he had experienced while the shaman and his cronies did their worst to stop him.

No one paid Bhim to be a missionary. He never received a salary to be a pastor or Christian worker. But like Baju and Darima, like the apostles Peter, Paul, and John, he was compelled by the love of God.

He had suffered immensely, yet it was abundantly clear that if called upon, he was ready to do it all over again... for his friend, Jesus. His plans for a future, his desire for a bigger house or lands, had all but disappeared. They had literally been beaten out of him. In its place was the unmistakable peace and glory of Christ clearly seen in his countenance.

They overcame (Satan) by the blood
of the Lamb and by the word of
their testimony; they did not love
their lives so much as to shrink from death.
Revelation 12:11

—Postscript—

Over the years, we entertained a number of people in our home with experiences similar to Bhim's. These, the poor and uneducated, were regarded as the scum of the earth. They had been grossly mistreated by their government officials. Like an evil plague, they had been rejected by their fellow villagers. Many of them owned little more than the breath they breathed. But that too, they were ready to expend so that the glory of Christ might continue to live in them.

We felt honored beyond words to have these brave, simple souls eat at our table and sometimes even stay the night with us. We have long since lost track of Bhim. In my memory, he came to see us over the years maybe three or four times. He had no degrees and no theological training. He might have completed third grade because he could read, but likely not much more.

In the sense of being void of fear, Bhim was not fearless. Nevertheless, in fearful situations, the peace of God reigned in his heart. He had experienced the unsurpassing love that resides in the heart of Jesus. He knew the Father's heart and counted himself a sheep... a sheep prepared to be sacrificed. As a result, again and again he placed his feet on the narrow path of high faith and walked through the Valley of the Shadow of Death, following his Shepherd's voice.

Be faithful, even to the point of death,
and I will give you the crown of life.
Revelation 2:11

EPILOGUE

Not to us, O LORD, not to us
but to your Name be the glory.
Psalm 115:1

When we began putting this book together, we soon realized that we had far too many stories about God's power to fit into a modest-sized book. To begin with, we set aside almost everything that dates from 2003 onwards.

After the leopard attack in 2003, Scrawny and Bir Bahadur, along with a couple of others, faced off powerful demons in a teenage girl and delivered her. The Powers of Darkness were beginning to lose their iron grip over the Magar people. The power of the shamans was clearly weakening, sometimes to the extent that the demons even ridiculed them.

Concurrently, the power of the Christians was definitely increasing, and the more the shamans' power to heal and deliver declined, the more the villagers came to the Christians for help. We were told that a few times the shamans simply sent the afflicted person to the Christians to receive healing.

In 2007, Baju's grandson, Mailha, was working overseas in Malaysia when his wife, Tema, was overcome by demons. When her shaman grandfather could do no more, he sent her to the Christians in Arakhala. There, she was delivered from the demons and became a believer.

In 2009 Baju's grandson returned home from Malaysia, and soon he too became a follower of Jesus. A couple of months later, their neighbor, Gomati, was overcome by very strong demons. She was taken from her home on Peak-of-the-gods over to Arakhala Village where a powerful confrontation between the Christians and the demons ensued. The resulting deliverance happened in the middle of the village and was so dramatic it became a catalyst that led to many other villagers following Jesus.

If we write a sequel, we would include the story of Baju's grandson. We might tell about a powerful witch's family who have become believers. Then there is the lady who had suffered horribly for twenty years. She had only been able to walk on her hands and knees until Michael's buddy, Poap Bahadur, prayed for her. Now she climbs the mountain unaided to attend church. And we would surely tell of Tema, and how God demonstrated his great power and love to her, and many, many more like her.

They overcame (Satan) by the blood of the Lamb.
Revelation 12:11

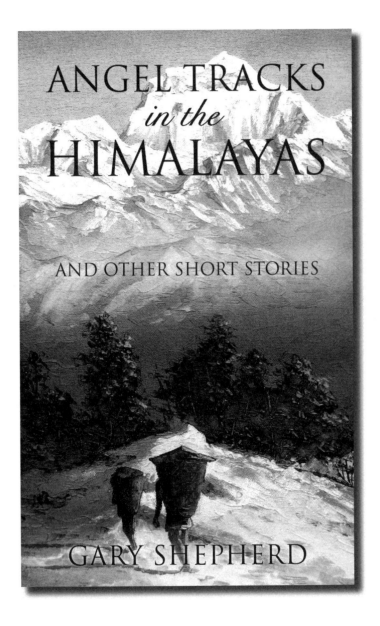

ANGEL TRACKS
in the
HIMALAYAS

AND OTHER SHORT STORIES

GARY SHEPHERD

In the U.S.A., copies of:
Angel Tracks in the Himalayas and
God's Hand in the Himalayas are available from the author. Multiple copies are available at discounted prices.

Author contact: garyshepherd3@gmail.com

Books are available in local bookstores and from Amazon.com. Look for them on Kindle and other eBooks soon.